fabulous party cakes and cupcakes

Matching Cakes and Cupcakes for Every Occasion

CAROL DEACON

TUTTLE Publishing

Tokyo | Rutland, Vermont | Singapore

Published by Tuttle Publishing, an imprint of
Periplus Editions (HK) Ltd

www.tuttlepublishing.com

Library of Congress Cataloging-in-Publication Data

Deacon, Carol.
 Fabulous party cakes and cupcakes : matching
designs for every occasion / Carol Deacon.
     p. cm.
 Includes index.
 ISBN 978-0-8048-4158-0 (hardcover)
1. Cake decorating. 2. Cupcakes. I. Title.
 TX771.2.D42698 2011
 641.8'6539--dc22
                            2010031801

ISBN 978-0-8048-4158-0

Distributed by
North America, Latin America & Europe
Tuttle Publishing
364 Innovation Drive
North Clarendon, VT 05759-9436 U.S.A.
Tel: 1 (802) 773-8930; Fax: 1 (802) 773-6993
info@tuttlepublishing.com
www.tuttlepublishing.com

Japan
Tuttle Publishing
Yaekari Building, 3rd Floor
5-4-12 Osaki
Shinagawa-ku
Tokyo 141-0032
Tel: (81) 3 5437-0171; Fax: (81) 3 5437-0755
sales@tuttle.co.jp
www.tuttle.co.jp

Asia Pacific
Berkeley Books Pte. Ltd.
61 Tai Seng Avenue #02-12
Singapore 534167
Tel: (65) 6280-1330; Fax: (65) 6280-6290
inquiries@periplus.com.sg
www.periplus.com

15 14 13 12 11   8 7 6 5 4 3 2
1104CP
Printed in Singapore

For June, Pam and Pauline. Three sisters who laugh, bicker, love and support each other and also enjoy a good cake!

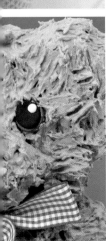

Contents

Introduction

When I first started baking cakes, which feels like a hundred years ago now, not everything went according to plan. I remember a large chocolate cake that I hadn't cooked for long enough and it had sunk in the center. I scooped the middle out and for reasons that escape me now, covered the whole sorry mess with canary yellow colored glacé icing. It must have looked dreadful.

I mention this because it saddens me when I hear from a number of people that they love my cakes but could never attempt to make one themselves. As I've just admitted—the quality of my early cakes wasn't that good either.

So the first secret behind creating wonderful cakes is now revealed: It's actually trying it in the first place. Sure, there may be some disasters along the way, but you will still learn from your mistakes. (I'll certainly never cover a chocolate cake with canary yellow glacé icing again!)

The second secret, I believe, is time. If you lead a busy life and can't for one minute imagine how you are going to find enough hours in the day to create the Happy Hamsters Cake your five-year-old is demanding, read the instructions before you start and spend a few moments working out how you can help yourself. Is there anything on the cake you can make early to save a mad rush before the party? You could, for instance, make the hamsters well in advance. You could also bake the sponge cake and freeze it to save time later. You could even make the cake a party activity and have the children make their own hamsters. But if you do what most of us do, which is to leave it all until the last minute and have an enormous stressful panic, you'll be pleased to know I've included a relatively quick and easy cupcake alternative for all the cakes.

Many of the cakes involve the use of rolled fondant sugarpaste. If you don't like this, then substitute it with marzipan instead. Jump in and give it a try—I think you'll be amazed!

Fondant wishes!

Carol Deacon

Basic Equipment

There is a vast amount of cake decorating equipment available these days. Here are some of the basics to get you started:

1. Cooling Rack You'll place your cakes on this once they have been baked and removed from the pan. This way the air is able to get all around the cake allowing for a faster cool down.

2. Cupcake Baking Tray These hollow molds hold the cupcake cases steady and stop the mixture from pushing the cases out of shape as the cupcakes bake.

3. Rolling Pins A large rolling pin is essential for rolling out the fondant for covering a cake. A small one is useful for rolling out small amounts, but you can also use a paintbrush if you don't have a small rolling pin.

4. Mixing Bowl

5. Sieve (or sifter) Used for sieving lumps out of flour and confectioners' sugar

6. Spatula Extremely useful for clearing the last of the mixture out of the mixing bowl.

7. Wooden Spoon Use for beating cake mixture by hand.

8. Turntable Although not essential, this really does make decorating cakes easier. I have had mine for years.

9. Scales There are all sorts of scales available. The ones shown are electronic but any type of scale will do. You'll use them for measuring out cake ingredients and fondant.

10. Cutters There are thousands of cutter designs available. I have found that a simple leaf and flower cutter are the ones

I mostly use but just buy them as you go along and only if you need them because they can be quite expensive.

11. Scissors You'll need a good sharp pair of scissors for cutting out greaseproof paper for lining baking tins, cutting ribbon and templates.

12. Tape Measure It's always handy to have one of these around to measure the circumference of boards and pans and measuring ribbon.

13. Baking Pan (Tin)

14. Cake Smoother Although not essential these will give your cakes a flat professional finish. Use them to iron out lumps and bumps on your cake's surface.

15. Measuring Cups If you cook using cup measurements you will need a set of these. There are many Internet sites that will convert cup measurements for different ingredients easily to grams or ounces if you need to adapt a recipe.

16. Fabric Pastry Piping Bag and Large Piping Nozzle (Tip) For piping butter-cream onto cupcakes.

17. Carving Knife

18. Palette Knife It is much easier to use a flexible palette knife to spread butter-cream around your cake than trying to do it using a normal kitchen knife.

19. Bone Tool A useful tool for making small hollows in fondant models.

20. Small, Sharp, Non-Serrated Knife Absolutely essential for cutting fondant sugarpaste cleanly.

21. Circle Cutters These may be a bit pricey, but I have found a set of these incredibly useful to have. It saves you hunting around the kitchen for something circular that's the right size.

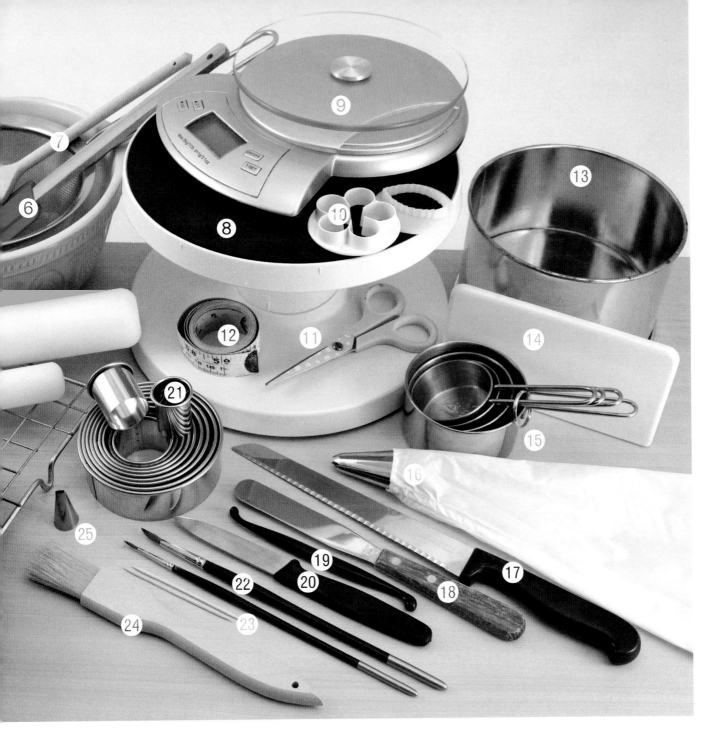

22. Paintbrushes Fine and medium paint-brushes are essential. Try to buy soft ones as some nylon brushes can be a bit hard and mark the fondant sugarpaste as you're using them. Keep your cake decorating paintbrushes separate from the ones the kids use for painting!

23. Toothpicks (Cocktail Sticks) Cheap and very useful. Use them for adding food color to fondant and rolling over fondant to make frills. Please don't put them inside models to provide support, in case an un-suspecting recipient bites into the model. Use a strand of raw, uncooked spaghetti instead.

24. Pastry Brush Useful when you need to dab water on cake boards. You can also use them to brush confectioners' sugar off models.

25. Piping Nozzle (Tip) As well as using these for piping decorations, I use them as mini circle cutters and for pressing scales or smiles into fondant characters.

Baking Your Cake

Making a basic sponge cake is really very simple and can be quite rewarding. Not only can you be confident that you are feeding your family and friends something that will taste great, but also your house will smell wonderfully warm, homey and inviting as it bakes. If you are baking a cake for a really important occasion and are using a new recipe for the first time, have a trial run first. If the cake turns out perfectly then great—freeze the cake and use it at the party. If you're not happy with the result then you have time to try again. The other thing worth mentioning is that if you already use a sponge cake recipe that you're familiar with and that works for you, feel free to use that. It may sound obvious, but you are not limited to just using my recipes under your icing.

Flour

I always use self-raising flour in my cakes, which is widely available. However, I know that flours vary depending on where you live so a similar type of product might be marketed in your area as self-rising or cake flour. Basically, it's flour that already has a rising agent added to it. It is very easy to make your own if none of the above are available by using plain flour (all-purpose flour):

Mix 1 1/2 teaspoons baking powder into 1 cup (150 g) of plain (all purpose) flour. Double or triple these amounts depending upon how much flour you need for your recipe. (There is also a huge amount of information on the Internet about flours in different countries, which is worth looking at if you are at all unsure.)

Sugar

When it comes to sugar, I tend to use superfine (caster) sugar when baking. This is ordinary white sugar that has been ground longer than granulated sugar to produce finer granules, this is supposed to lead to a lighter cake when baked. I have used granulated sugar though in the past and the end result tasted just fine, so don't panic if you've only got granulated sugar in your cupboard. It is possible to make your own superfine sugar if you wish. Simply place some sugar into a food processor and give it a quick blast for about 30 seconds.

Lining the Pan

This might seem nit-picky, but it's worth doing to prevent your cake from sticking to the inside of your pan. Grease the inside of your pan by rubbing a little butter around it (this will hold the paper in place). Cut a piece of waxed paper long enough to go around the sides of the pan and that will just stand higher than the top of your pan. Stand the pan on top of another piece of waxed paper and draw around it. Cut out the shape by cutting inside the drawn line. Stand the long strip around the inside of the pan and place the base section inside.

Alternative Liners

You can buy ready-shaped pan liners for round, square and loaf pans but as these usually come in packs of 50, so it's quite an expensive way of doing things unless you make a large number of cakes. There are also a number of cake release sprays on the market now. As the name suggests, you spray these onto the pan before filling with cake mixture and bake as normal. When the cake is baked, you simply tip the cake out and the spray releases it from the pan. These are extremely useful for oddly shaped novelty pans with awkward nooks and crannies that make lining them with waxed paper impossible.

Odd-sized Cakes

Here's an easy way to calculate how much cake mixture you need if you're ever asked for an odd-sized cake that isn't covered here or you need to bake a cake in an unusually shaped pan.

For Larger Pans

1 Take a cake pan that you have used before and for which you know how much cake mixture it holds, then fill it two-thirds full of water.
2 Tip it into the pan that you are planning to use.
3 Repeat, counting the number of times you need to do it until the new pan is two-thirds full.
4 If the number of times you need to pour water into the pan is double the number needed to fill your usual pan you know that you need to make double the amount of cake mixture. If the larger pan takes three times as much, triple the amount of cake mixture.

For Smaller Pans

1 Fill the small pan that you plan to use two-thirds full with water.
2 Tip this into a pan that you have used before and for which you know how much cake mixture you would need.
3 Continue to tip water from the smaller pan into the larger until the larger one is two-thirds full.
4 If you needed to empty the small pan three times then you know you need to make a third of the amount of cake mixture that you would use for the bigger one so divide the amounts by three and so on.

Lining a pan

TIPS FOR STORING AND FREEZING: Once cooled, you should decorate your cake as soon as possible. If you cannot decorate it right away or you prefer to work with the cake the next day when the crumb is firmer, then let it cool down completely. When it is cool, wrap it in plastic wrap overnight. When doing this, I tend to leave it in the greaseproof paper.

Once the cake is coated in buttercream or with fondant, then the sponge is airtight. Keep it in a cardboard cake box to keep dust and insects off it and keep it somewhere cool (not in a refrigerator if you used fondant sugarpaste) until required. Don't use an airtight plastic container with fondant or your cake will sweat.

Both the Madeira and chocolate cake should be eaten within four days.

Both the chocolate and Madeira cakes will freeze beautifully. Allow them to cool after baking, then bind them in plastic wrap and place in the freezer. They will keep for up to three months. To defrost, remove them from the freezer and allow them to defrost at room temperature for a few hours.

Basic Madeira Sponge Cake Recipe

This is a simple all-in-one recipe. I cook my Madeira Cake on a lower heat than most other Madeira recipes. This means that it will take longer to cook, but the center will not rise into quite such a high dome while baking.

Madeira Sponge Cake Ingredients Amounts

For Square Pans	6-inch 15 cm	7-inch 18 cm	8-inch 20 cm	9-inch 23 cm	10-inch 25 cm	11-inch 28 cm	12-inch 30 cm
For Round Pans	6-inch 15 cm	7-inch 18 cm	8-inch 20 cm	9-inch 23 cm	10-inch 25 cm	11-inch 28 cm	12-inch 30 cm
Self-rising Flour	1½ cups 170 g	2 cups 225 g	2¾ cups 340 g	3½ cups 450 g	4 cups 500 g	4½ cups 570 g	5 cups 625 g	6 cups 735 g
Butter	½ cup 1 stick 115 g	¾ cup 1½ sticks 170 g	1¼ cups 2½ sticks 285 g	1¾ cups 3½ sticks 400 g	2 cups 4 sticks 450 g	2¼ cups 4½ sticks 500 g	2½ cups 5 sticks 575 g	3 cups 6 sticks 685 g
Sugar	½ cup 115 g	¾ cup 170 g	1¼ cups 285 g	1¾ cups 400 g	2 cups 450 g	2¼ cups 500 g	2½ cups 565 g	3 cups 680g
Eggs	2	3	5	7	8	9	10	12
Milk	1 tbsp	1 tbsp	2 tbsps	3 tbsps	4 tbsps	5 tbsps	5 tbsps	6 tbsps
Baking Time	1 hr	1–1½ hrs	1½–2 hrs	1½–2¼ hrs	2 hrs	2 hrs	2–2½ hrs	2–2½ hrs

1 Grease and line your cake pan and preheat your oven to 300° F (150° C).

2 If you are using a mixer, sift your flour into the bowl and add the rest of the ingredients. Start the mixer on its slowest speed and gently bind the ingredients together. Switch to the mixer's highest speed and beat all the ingredients together for a minute until the mixture is pale and smooth.

3 If you are mixing by hand, make sure your butter is very soft (place it in a microwave for a few seconds if necessary). Then beat the butter and sugar together until creamy. Add the eggs and beat those in until the mixture is smooth. Sift the flour and gently stir it in with a metal spoon.

4 Spoon the mixture into your prepared pan and smooth the top. Place the cake in the center of the pre-heated oven and bake for the required time. Not all ovens bake the same, so the baking times provided are approximate. Your cake will be ready when it is starting to pull away from the sides and you can't hear bubbling noises. To check for sure, insert a knife or metal skewer and if it comes out clean then the cake is done. If there's mixture on the skewer, cook for another ten minutes or so.

Variations

Vary the taste, color and even texture of this recipe by stirring in a tablespoon of cocoa or coffee for a simple chocolate or coffee cake; add almond or mint flavoring, desiccated coconut, a ripe banana (mashed) or the zest of a lemon or orange. If you want more color, stir in a little food coloring before you begin baking. If you just stir it in lightly, your cake will have a marbled appearance. You can alter the texture by mixing in chocolate beans or chips, raisins or sliced glacé cherries.

TIP: If you are making a large 12-inch (30 cm) cake and don't possess a large mixing bowl, you may find it easier to halve the ingredients and mix them up in two lots. Gently stir them together in the baking pan.

Basic Chocolate Cake Recipe

This is my favorite cake. Not only does it have a rich taste, but it has a strong velvety texture that is both easy to cut and holds its shape well (important if you are carving the cake into an unusual shape). It also keeps extremely well. For a party on a Saturday, you could bake the cake on a Wednesday allowing you a good two days to decorate it. It is a bit of a fussy cake to put together, but you can make things easier for yourself by weighing out the ingredients and separating the whites and the yolks of the eggs before you start. You will need to use a mixer. For a less complicated chocolate cake, use the Madeira cake recipe but add some cocoa powder to it.

Chocolate Cake Ingredients Amount

For Square Pans	6-inch 15 cm	7-inch 18 cm	8-inch 20 cm	9-inch 23 cm	10-inch 25 cm	11-inch 28 cm	12-inch 30 cm
For Round Pans	6-inch 15 cm	7-inch 18 cm	8-inch 20 cm	9-inch 23 cm	10-inch 25 cm	11-inch 28 cm	12-inch 30 cm
Semisweet Chocolate	150 g	175 g	225 g	275 g	350 g	400 g	450 g	500 g
Butter	$1/3$ cup $3/4$ stick 90 g	$1/2$ cup 1 stick 115 g	$3/4$ cup $1 1/2$ sticks 175 g	1 cup 2 sticks/ 225 g	$1 1/4$ cups $2 1/2$ sticks 285 g	$1 1/2$ cups 3 sticks 350 g	$1 3/4$ cups $3 1/2$ sticks 400 g	2 cups 4 sticks 450 g
Sugar (superfine)	$1/5$ cup 40 g	$1/3$ cup 75 g	$1/2$ cup 115 g	$2/3$ cup 150 g	$3/4$ cup 175 g	$9/10$ cup 200 g	1 cup 225 g	$1 1/5$ cups 250 g
Eggs (separated)	3	4	6	8	10	12	14	16
Self-rising Flour	$3/5$ cup 75 g	$9/10$ cup 115 g	$1 1/4$ cups 175 g	$1 4/5$ cups 225 g	$2 1/4$ cups 285 g	$2 3/4$ cups 350 g	$3 1/4$ cups 400 g	$3 3/4$ cups 450 g
Confectioners' Sugar (icing)	$1/5$ cup 25 g	$1/3$ cup 45 g	$1/2$ cup 50 g	$2/3$ cup 75 g	$3/4$ cup 100 g	$1 1/10$ cups 130 g	$1 1/5$ cups 145 g	$1 1/3$ cups 170 g
Baking Time	45 mins	45 mins–1 hr	1 hr	1–$1 1/4$ hrs	1–$1 1/4$ hrs	$1 1/4$–$1 1/2$ hrs	$1 1/4$–$1 3/4$ hrs	$1 1/4$–2 hrs

1 Pre-heat your oven to 350° F (180° C). Line your cake pan. Separate the eggs placing the whites and yolks in two different bowls.

2 Melt the chocolate (see Melting Chocolate section, page 17) in a large bowl and place to one side.

3 Beat the butter and sugar together using your mixer until fluffy.

4 Beat in the egg yolks. Tip the melted chocolate into the mixture and mix on a slower speed. Keep the bowl of melted chocolate nearby.

5 Gently stir the sifted flour into the mixture using a metal spoon. Once mixed, tip it all into the bowl of melted chocolate. Remove the beater from the mixer.

6 Wash out your machine's mixing bowl. Dry it and place the egg whites into it.

7 Place the whisking element on your mixer. Beat the egg whites until stiff, then beat in the confectioners' sugar (icing). Remove the whisk and put the beater back on.

8 Tip the chocolate mixture into the egg whites and mix together on a slow speed. It will look dreadful at first but the two will eventually mix smoothly together.

9 Scrape the mixture into the prepared pan and bake immediately.

10 When the cake is ready it should be silent, that is, no bubbling noises. To be absolutely sure, insert a knife or metal skewer. (You may have to cut a small chunk out of the cake's crust to do this). If it comes out clean then the cake is done. If there's mixture on the skewer, cook for a little longer.

TIP: The cake will form a hard crust on top as it bakes and you may find that it scorches and/or cracks. This is normal. Slice the crust off once the cake has cooled just before you buttercream it.

Unless you have a very big mixer you will find it easier to make the largest sizes in two separate batches then gently stir together. Have everything weighed out beforehand though as this mixture cannot sit around too long before baking.

Using Heatproof Glass Bowls and Loaf Pans

A one pound loaf pan and one pint heatproof pudding bowl are used to make the cakes for "Smelly Sneaker" and "Chocolate Teddy Bear."

1 Use a 2-egg Madeira mixture from the chart on page 14 for the pint bowl (you will need to make two) and a 3-egg mixture for the loaf pan.
2 Grease the inside of the bowl or pan by rubbing a little butter around it by using a bit of kitchen paper. Cut out a small greaseproof disc for the bowl and lay that in the bottom or a small greaseproof strip for the loaf pan and lay that on the base.
3 Make up the mixture as normal and fill either item two-thirds full. If you find you have too much, use the excess to make a few cupcakes.
4 Cook for about 45 minutes until the mixture seems to be pulling away from the sides. If it's silent and not bubbling it's done. Let it cool for a few minutes then slide a palette knife around the edges to help release the cake.
5 Turn the cake over and tip onto a cooling rack to cool down. Remove the greaseproof paper before decorating.

Microwave Cakes

It is perfectly possible to bake a cake in a microwave as long as you don't use a metal pan. They do not brown on top so they look a little anemic and the texture is slightly drier, but they cook in 4 minutes so microwave cakes definitely have the environmental advantage. The amounts here are for a 7-inch (18 cm)-round microwave cake pan or a $1/2$-quart ($1/2$-liter) heatproof pudding bowl.

Microwave Vanilla Sponge

$1/2$ cup butter (1 stick/120 g)
$1/2$ cup superfine (caster) sugar (120 g)
2 large eggs
1 teaspoon vanilla extract
$3/4$ cup self-rising flour (120 g)
$1/2$ teaspoon baking powder

1 Grease the pan or bowl and place a disc of greaseproof paper in the base.
2 Beat the butter and sugar together until creamy.
3 Beat in the eggs and vanilla.
4 Sift the flour and baking powder together and stir in.
5 Scrape into the prepared pan and bake on full power for four minutes.
6 Leave to stand for about 10 minutes then slide a knife around the edges of the pan and turn the cake out.

Microwave Chocolate Sponge

$1/2$ cup butter (1 stick/120 g)
$1/2$ cup superfine (caster) sugar (120 g)
2 large eggs
$2/3$ cup self-rising flour (90 g)
2 tablespoons cocoa powder
$1/2$ teaspoon baking powder

1 Follow steps 1–3 for the Microwave Vanilla Sponge recipe above leaving out the vanilla extract.
2 Sift the flour, baking powder, and cocoa powder together into the mixture and gently stir in. Then follow steps 5 and 6 of the Microwave Vanilla Sponge recipe.

Making Leftover Truffles

I've featured these little fellows before, but they're such a cute way of using up the leftover cake you get when you slice bits off the top of a cake to level it. (Besides it gave me another opportunity to make some and test a few—purely for research purposes, of course!)

Crumble the leftover bits of cake in a bowl and weigh it. You will then need about 1 oz (30 g) of any type of chocolate (milk, semi-sweet [plain] or white) to every 1 oz (30 g) of cake crumbs. So, if you have 4 oz (120 g) of crumbs you need 4 oz (120 g) of chocolate.

Melt the chocolate and stir it into the cake crumbs then roll it into little ball shapes. Delicious plain but better if decorated with melted chocolate, sprinkles or a little sieved cocoa or confectioners' sugar. Place a few in a box and you have a sweet little gift for someone or a neat homemade wedding favor.

Using Stock Syrup

I am often contacted by people who, for one reason or another, have to bake a cake a few days earlier than they'd like to and are anxious that the cake will dry out before it is eaten, so I thought I'd include this recipe for stock syrup. Stock syrup is basically sugar dissolved in water that is dabbed onto the cake before fondant is applied and therefore adds extra moisture to the cake.

1 Pour ¹/₂ cup (100 g) superfine sugar and ²/₃ cup (150 ml) water into a saucepan and stir together.
2 Boil and simmer for about 5 minutes until the sugar has dissolved. (Alternatively, you could place the sugar and water in a heat-proof bowl and microwave for a couple of minutes until the sugar is dissolved.)
3 Allow the mixture to cool.

How to Use Stock Syrup
When you are ready to ice your cake, slice the cake horizontally as normal, but before spreading buttercream onto the layers, dab some stock syrup over each slice using a soft pastry brush. Dab it lightly all over but don't saturate the sponge. Spread butter cream over the layers and assemble your cake as normal. You can flavor the syrup with liqueur—a dash of rum works really well with chocolate cake, but should be avoided if you're making the cake for children!

Melting Chocolate

To melt chocolate, break it into squares and place it into a heatproof bowl. Then place it on top of a saucepan of gently simmering water and allow it to melt. The base of the bowl should not be in the water. Do not allow any water to splash into the chocolate or it will turn gritty and unuseable. The other, and probably more convenient method, is to place the broken chocolate in a heatproof, non-metallic bowl and use a microwave. Heat it on full power for about a minute. Stir it and repeat again until the chocolate has melted. The chocolate will burn if you overdo it, so it's better to do it in short bursts and check it rather than setting the timer for five minutes and wondering why there's an awful smell of burning after three minutes have passed.

Making Your Cupcakes

The humble cupcake has the uncanny skill of being able to grace any party. From the mayhem of a kid's birthday party to a society wedding, the cupcake is a good fit for every type of occasion. They're easy to make, fun to decorate, and everyone loves them.

Basic Cupcake Recipe

There is simply not enough space here to write down all the cupcake recipes available (type "cupcake recipes" into a search engine on your computer and you'll see what I mean), so for the sake of space and forests everywhere, we'll keep things simple. For all the cupcakes in this book I use the Madeira recipe on page 14.

The 2-egg mixture will make approximately 12 cupcakes. So double the amounts if you need more.

1 Pre-heat your oven to 300° F (150° C) and stand the cupcake liners in a baking tray.
2 Mix up the cake batter as instructed. It should be pale in color and very soft.
3 Put two teaspoons of batter into the cupcake liners. Take a spoonful of mixture on one, place it over an empty cupcake liner, and use the second spoon to push it in. This prevents your hands from getting sticky.
4 When all the cases are filled, place the tray into the oven and bake for about 25 minutes or until the cakes are golden and springy to the touch.

Variations
All the flavor variations given on page 14 for a larger Madeira cake will work their delicious magic on cupcakes too. So have a look at the list if you prefer something other than plain.

Patch, Ginger and Lily enjoy a picnic of mini-cupcakes (see page 43) in the sunshine

Cupcake Liners Before we get onto the fancy decorating section, a quick word about cupcake liners. Once upon a time you could only get white paper ones. This wasn't a problem because we only wanted white paper ones...until someone invented colored ones and now, well, the range of cupcake case colors and patterns is huge and will match any party color theme. You can still get white though!

Silicon Liners Recently, silicon has come to the party and it's possible to buy re-useable silicon cupcake cases that you can use over and over again. These are bright, breezy and won't lose their shape or color. Use them in exactly the same way you would paper cake liners.

Decorating Your Cupcakes

There are many ways to decorate a cupcake. Glacé icing (a mixture of water and confectioners' sugar) is probably the easiest method of all. Top it with a glacé cherry and it becomes a simple classic. For the most part I have tried to keep things simple and have just used plain buttercream. The recipes for buttercream is on page 22 and the glacé icing recipe is below.

I have piped buttercream onto many of the cupcakes but if you don't have any piping equipment, then just use a teaspoon to place a satisfying dollop on top of your cupcake instead. There are two main reasons why I choose to use piping:

A They look neat and photograph nicely

B I bought a new decorating set that had a big fat star shaped piping tip, and I just found it really satisfying to use. (I know—I should go out more!)

Glacé Icing

This is probably the simplest frosting of all and is easily done by hand. This should be enough to cover 12 cupcakes or the top of a 7-inch (18 cm) cake so double the amounts given if you need more.

1 cup confectioners' sugar (125 g)
1 tablespoon water

Sift the sugar into a bowl. Add the water and stir together. If it is too thick, add a little more water one drop at a time. Substitute lemon juice for the water for a sweet alternative with a tangy kick.

Piping Your Cupcakes

I would recommend using a nylon-pastry bag for piping frosting onto your cupcakes. It is possible to make your own out of greaseproof paper, but the problem is that you are trying to force a large quantity of buttercream through a large piping tip and greaseproof paper has a tendency to tear. Using a greaseproof paper bag does have one advantage though—no greasy bag to wash up afterwards.

1 Use the largest star-nozzle (tip) you can find and place it into the bag.
2 Stand the bag in a glass or your left hand (right hand if you're left handed) and fold the top of the bag over to form a cuff.
3 Using a palette knife, place two or three large dollops of buttercream inside the bag. Clasp the palette knife through the bag and slide the knife out. Twist the end to close the bag and force the buttercream down into the tip.

4 Pipe around the outside edge of the cupcake. Then continue with a lesser spiral around the cupcake repeatedly until the whole of the top of the cake is covered.
5 To release the nozzle, press the tip lightly into the center of the cake and pull upwards. The icing should break away leaving a pointed star in the center.

TIP: To clean the bag afterwards, turn it inside out and scrape off as much buttercream as you can using a spatula or palette knife. Then wash in hot soapy water, rinse and allow to dry. Don't be tempted to just run it under the hot tap to remove the buttercream as the fat will solidify once it's cooled and you'll end up with blocked drains.

Using a Nylon-Pastry Bag for Piping Your Cupcakes

Using Cupcake Wrappers

These little gems will enhance any cupcake. Basically they are laser-cut designer sleeves that you stand your cupcake in. They come in all sorts of colors and designs. I used butterfly ones on "Chocolate Butterfly Cupcakes" on page 36.

1 To use, bake your cupcakes in standard paper cupcake liners and decorate them.

2 Assemble the wrapper and stand the cupcake in the middle.

3 If you find yourself getting sticky placing the cake inside the wrapper, assemble the wrapper and slide it over a small jar. I found that a spice jar is the ideal size. Stand the cupcake on top of the jar and lift the cupcake wrapper upwards. It will automatically lift the cupcake off the jar and into the right position within the wrapper.

4 Don't even attempt to try to cut corners by spooning cake mixture into the wrappers and baking it because they don't have a base and it will just be a mess. I wouldn't even try removing the cupcake liner before placing it inside the wrapper because the cupcake liner helps keep the cake fresh.

Edible Paper Flowers Cupcakes

Chocolate Butterfly Cupcakes

How to Apply Your Cupcake Wrappers

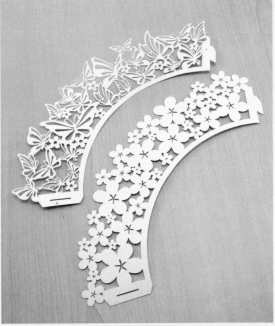

Coating Your Cake with Buttercream

I use a very simple and versatile buttercream recipe to both coat my cakes prior to covering them with fondant or for decorating them with piping. It is also easy to vary the color and taste to match or enhance your design.

Basic Buttercream Recipe

These are the amounts for what I have referred to in the instructions for the cake designs in this book as "1 quantity." If you are making a big cake you can double or triple the amounts. You can also make it ahead of when you need it. If covered, it will keep in the refrigerator for a week or can be frozen for up to a month.

1 cup softened butter (2 sticks/250 g)
4 cups confectioners' sugar (500 g)
1 teaspoon vanilla extract
1 tablespoon hot water

1 Beat the butter until soft and creamy.
2 Add the rest of the ingredients. Bind together slowly then beat fast until the mixture is light and fluffy. If you are using a mixer and you let it beat the icing for 5–10 minutes you will find it turns the buttercream almost white. It is possible to do this by hand but you'll need big muscles! If the mixture is hard and unworkable, add a little more water. If it gets too sloppy, add more sugar.
3 Scrape the buttercream into an airtight container and cover until needed. Store in the refrigerator.

Making your mark
(see TIP on page 23.)

Flavoring and Coloring the Buttercream

There are many ways to alter the taste of the buttercream. Here are just a few. If you add too much of anything and the icing becomes too runny, just add more sugar.

Chocolate Buttercream

1 To make a rich chocolate buttercream stir $3\frac{1}{2}$ ounces (100 g) of melted semi-sweet (plain) chocolate into the buttercream. You can also use white or milk chocolate to produce a lighter, sweeter buttercream.
2 Alternatively, mix 1 tablespoon of cocoa powder into a paste with 1–2 tablespoons of hot water and stir it in.

Coffee Buttercream

Mix 1 tablespoon of instant coffee into 1 tablespoon of hot water and add to the buttercream.

Fruit Buttercream

Mix a couple of tablespoons of jam into the buttercream, it will add a fruity flavor and color it as well.

Other Flavorings

There are many commercial flavorings available—peppermint, almond and lemon to name but a few. A few drops are all you need to add a tasty tang.

Adding Chocolate Chips

I mixed a handful of chocolate chips into the buttercream on a simple sponge cake the other day that, according to a nine-year-old neighbor who sampled a slice, elevated the cake from being one of my "ordinary boring ones" to "the best cake ever!"

Coloring the Buttercream

Some flavorings such as chocolate, coffee and a dollop of strawberry jam will automatically alter the color of the buttercream. You can also stir in a little food coloring of your choice if you want. Try to use paste or gel colors because liquid colors may make the icing too runny.

Coating the Cake

I like to use buttercream to coat my cakes prior to covering them with rolled fondant. The buttercream acts as "glue" to hold it firmly to the sponge. Jam can be used, especially apricot jam because its flavor is not too overpowering.

Place your cake onto the cake board and spread buttercream around the sides first. This means you can hold the top steady with your other hand without getting too sticky (a turntable makes doing this much easier). Once the sides are covered, spread buttercream over the top.

TIP: You've sliced the cake, filled it with buttercream and re-assembled it but what on earth's happened? It doesn't seem to want to go back together the same way. If that's ever happened to you then here's a clever way to stop it from happening again.

To prepare your cake for filling by making sure that the top is level. Slice a little off the top if necessary—especially if it has cracked, scorched or risen up into a dome while baking. Then turn the cake upside down so that what was once the base now forms a nice flat top.

Now, before you cut it, put a little buttercream on your palette knife and make a vertical mark on the side of the cake.

Slice the cake into two or three layers.

Spread a layer of buttercream over the top of the first layer and place the second layer on top, lining the buttercream marks up together. Repeat with the top layer. If the buttercream marks all line up, your layers should all fit back together neatly.

TIP : This is a neat trick to stop crumbs from getting mixed up in your buttercream, this is especially annoying if you are just coating the cake with buttercream and not planning to use rolled fondant later.

Cover the cake as above with a thin buttercream coating then place it in the refrigerator for twenty minutes or longer—until the buttercream has hardened and the cake feels solid.

Take it out of the refrigerator and spread on a second buttercream coating. Those offensive crumbs should now be held in check by the first hardened layer of buttercream.

It's a Wrap!

I find that once I've coated my cake with buttercream and it's ready for covering with rolled fondant, my work area is usually such a sticky crumb buttercream disaster zone that there's usually at least a 15 minute delay while I try and clear the decks. To prevent the buttercream from drying out and losing its ability to hold the fondant in place securely, I cover the cake with plastic wrap and remove it just before I'm about to cover the cake. It also means that it won't matter if you're suddenly distracted by the phone ringing or a small child falling over and requiring "urgent" medical attention for a bump on their knee, the buttercream on the cake will still be ready when you are ready.

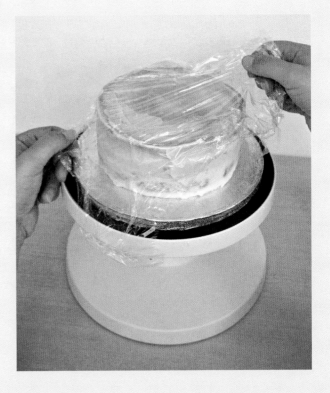

Working with Fondant Icing Paste

Fondant is also known under different names, as such as sugarpaste, ready-to-roll icing, and plastic icing (don't worry there's no plastic in it!). It is a very easy and versatile medium to use. It's a bit like using edible modeling clay and can be used for both covering cakes and making models. You can usually find fondant in supermarkets in the home baking aisle or at cake decorating shops. It can also be ordered online. Different brands may vary slightly, but most perform virtually the same. It is also possible to make your own. If you prefer, you could use marzipan instead of fondant.

Basic Fondant Recipe

4 cups confectioners' sugar (500 g)
1 egg white or equivalent dried egg white (meringue powder) reconstituted
2 tablespoons corn syrup (this is available from cake decorating shops and some drugstores and supermarkets)

1 Sieve the sugar into a large bowl and make a well in the center.
2 Pour the egg white and corn syrup into the center and stir in.
3 Use your hands to finish kneading the fondant together. It should feel silky and smooth.
4 Double wrap the fondant in two plastic food bags to prevent it from drying out until you need to use it. If you want you can use it immediately and it does not need to be kept in the refrigerator, but use it within a week.

Basic Rules

There are a few fundamental rules that you need to know when working with fondant:

1 It will dry out when exposed to air, so it is important to keep unused fondant tightly wrapped in small plastic food bags in a plastic container with a lid. It does not need to be refrigerated.
2 You will need to have a bowl of confectioners' sugar nearby. You will use this for rolling the fondant out on and for preventing your fingers from getting too sticky.
3 Stick your models together by using cooled, boiled water applied with a soft medium paintbrush. You can also use the brush as a tool for picking up small items such as eyes and ears. The paintbrush can also be used as a mini-rolling pin if you need a small flat piece of fondant.
4 You will get a few dusty confectioners' sugar marks on your cake and models as you work. Resist the temptation to deal with them right away and wait until you have finished your cake. Then you can wipe the marks away with a soft damp paintbrush. The fondant will be shiny for a while but will eventually revert to a matte finish.
5 If you drip water onto the fondant, wipe it off immediately or it will dissolve the sugar in the icing and leave an unsightly hollow.
6 Try to make up the colors of fondant that you know you are going to need before you start decorating.
7 In many of the step shots I have shown "exploded" figures to try and explain visually the shapes I have used to construct the models. **Don't make all the components before you start.** Make up the individual pieces and stick them in place as you go along. Otherwise the smaller parts will start to dry out and crack.
8 Use light dabs of cooled, boiled water to stick your models together. Don't soak them or the bits you're trying to stick on will simply slide off.

Covering the Cake

You need to soften the fondant first to make it easier to roll out and use. To do this, knead it on a clean work surface dusted with confectioners' sugar to prevent it from sticking. Alternatively, you can microwave it for 15–20 seconds. (Don't go mad with the microwave or it will melt!) At this stage, the actual cake you plan to cover should be buttercreamed and ready.

1 Roll the fondant out using a rolling pin to flatten it to a thickness of about 1/4 inch (5mm). Again, make sure you dust your work surface well with confectioners' sugar.

2 To place the fondant on the cake, you can either roll it loosely around your rolling pin as you would a pastry or you can carefully slide your hands, palms up, under the fondant and lift it keeping your hands flat. If you can feel that the fondant is sticking to your work surface, slide a palette knife under it to loosen it.

3 Lift and place the fondant over the top of your cake. Starting with the top of the cake to try and prevent air getting trapped underneath, smooth over the top of the cake with the flat of your hands. Then gently ease the sides into place and trim away any excess from around the base with a small, sharp, non-serrated knife.

Cake Smoothers

These are flat bits of plastic with handles that will help you achieve a smooth professional-looking finish. They are one piece of equipment I would strongly suggest you buy if you are serious about cake decorating. You use them like you would an iron. You run them over the top and sides to literally iron out any lumps and bumps.

Air Bubbles and Cracking

These happen to all of us at some time or another so don't despair. You're not alone.

1 To remove an air bubble that is trapped under your fondant, prick it with a clean dressmaker's pin held at an angle and gently press the air out.

2 Cracking on the edge of the cake can happen for a variety of reasons, the main one being that the fondant had started to dry out. This is why it is important to keep it covered when not in use. In some cases, gently rubbing over the crack with your fingertips may help. If you have covered the cake using white fondant then dipping your finger in icing sugar before rubbing the edges can help as the icing sugar fills the tiny cracks.

3 If the cracks are really offensive to you (and cake decorators are often very hard on themselves) and not just something that nobody else will notice then you'll have to take the "necessity is the mother of invention" route and cover them up with something. I find a trail of leaves can hide a multitude of sins!

Covering the Cake Board

There are various ways to cover a cake board, but if you're pushed for time, or don't have enough fondant, leave it plain and scatter a few sweets around it instead.

All-In-One Method

This is the easiest method. Moisten the cake board with a little water. Knead a ball of fondant until soft, and then roll it out into a thick, flattish circle. Place it onto the center of the board and continue to roll it out until it goes over the edges of the board. Run a cake smoother, if you have one, over the top for an extra flat finish and trim away the excess from the edges. You can then place an iced cake or a display of cupcakes on top of the covered board.

The Bandage Method

Your iced cake should be in position on the board. Lightly moisten the exposed cake board around the cake with a little water. Roll out and cut out a strip of fondant wider than the exposed board and long enough to go right around the cake. Cut a thin strip off one long edge of the strip to neaten it and slide your knife along under the strip to ensure it's not stuck to your work surface. Carefully roll the fondant up like a loose bandage, then with the neat edge up against the side of the cake, unwind it around the board. If you have one, run a cake smoother over the base and trim and neaten the joint and the edges.

Coloring the Fondant

You can buy ready colored fondant in an assortment of colors from cake decorating shops or online stores. It is also possible to color your own. To do this, it is best to use food color gels. These are thicker and more concentrated than liquid colors and because you will use far less, they won't alter the consistency of your icing as much as liquid colors will.

To color your fondant, apply a few dabs of food color paste with a toothpick that you can throw away afterwards. It's very tempting to stick your craft knife into the pot but try to avoid doing this to prevent contamination.

Then knead the color into the icing.

You can also knead different colored lumps of fondant together to achieve a different color. Knead a little bit of red into a lump of white to make pink for example.

If you are aiming for a marbled effect like the one I used on the Baby Dolphin Cake then stop kneading before the fondant becomes a flat matte color. If you put too much in, then knead some white fondant back in.

To get a solid block of color, continue kneading until the fondant is all one shade with no visible streaks.

Creating Flesh Tones

For a pinkish flesh color, I use a shade of food color paste called "paprika." Alternatively you can knead a little pink, yellow and white fondant together.

For darker tones, use brown food color gel or knead a little green, red and black fondant together.

Knead a little white fondant back in if you need to lighten it, or a little yellow if you want to alter the shade.

Birthday Cake Candles

When it comes to putting candles on a birthday cake, most of us use candles in little plastic holders, which is fine, but, if you have time, you can make the candle holders part of the actual design.

I have used fondant "pebbles" and "rocks" many times as candleholders. Also, thick flower and ball shapes work well.

You can even have your characters holding the candles. Position the character's hands over their head. Press a candle into a plastic candleholder and insert into the top of the character.

It's also worth looking out for novelty candles. Some, such as soccer balls and champagne bottles, could actually be incorporated into your design.

Just make sure that the candle is safe before lighting. It must stand straight and be secure and well away from anything that might catch fire.

Coloring Coconut and Sugar

Green-colored desiccated coconut makes excellent grass. To make it, place some coconut into a bowl and add a little food color gel then mix it in.

By using brown and black food color gel you can make realistic looking "gravel." You can also color sugar this way too.

If you are worried about staining your hands, wear a disposable plastic glove.

Baby Dolphin Cake

If you have never achieved a marbled-effect using fondant before you will be an expert after making this cake! The secret is to stop kneading the color in before the fondant turns into one flat color. Even if it does, all is not lost, simply knead a bit more white fondant back into the mix.

Ingredients

7 in (18 cm) round cake
1 quantity buttercream (see page 22)
1 lb 6 oz (650 g) white fondant
7 oz (200 g) gray-colored fondant
1/3 oz (10 g) brown fondant (see "Tips" below)
Blue and black food color gels
2–3 tablespoons soft brown sugar
Confectioners' sugar for rolling out fondant on
Water, boiled and cooled, for sticking

Equipment

10 in (25 cm) round board
Carving knife
Palette knife
Rolling pin
Cake smoothers (optional)
Small, sharp, non-serrated knife
Craft knife/scalpel (optional—see "Tip" below)
Medium and fine paintbrushes
Dolphin templates (see page 78)
3/4 in (2 cm) circle cutter (optional)
Piping nozzle (tip), any style
Teaspoon

> **TIPS:** Although not essential, it is much easier to cut around a template if you use a craft knife or scalpel because the blade is so much finer.
>
> If you don't have any brown fondant, knead in a little brown food coloring instead.

To Make Your Dolphin Cake

1 Level the cake and turn it upside down. Slice it horizontally and fill with buttercream. Reassemble the cake. Place it in the center of the cake board and spread buttercream over the top and sides.

2 Knead 1 pound 2 ounces (500 g) of white fondant until pliable. Apply a few dabs of blue food color gel and knead it into the fondant. It will not take long before you see a marbled-effect appearing. Stop before the fondant turns all one color. Roll the marbled fondant out and lift and place over the cake.

3 Smooth the fondant over the top and sides and trim and neaten around the base.

4 Dust your work surface with confectioners' sugar and knead and roll out the gray fondant to a thickness of about 1/8 inch (3 mm).

5 Holding your knife almost vertical, cut around the body template and stick on top of the cake with a little water.

6 Repeat the procedure adding the tail, mouth and fins. Press three lines into each tail section with the back of your knife. Keep the excess fondant for making rocks later.

7 To make the eye, thinly roll out about 1/3 ounce (10 g) of white fondant and using a 3/4-inch (2 cm) circle cutter or knife, cut out a flat disc for the eye, or make a 1/8-ounce (5 g) white ball and squash it. Roll the remaining white into small balls. Squash them and stick on top of the cake to look like bubbles.

8 Paint the pupil on the eye and a few eyelashes with black food color and a fine paintbrush.

9 To make the shells, partially knead 3 1/2 ounces (100 g) of white fondant and 1/3 ounce (10 g) of brown fondant together until a marbled-effect appears.

10 Pull off about 1/8 ounce (5 g) and roll into a ball. Squash and shape the ball to form a sort of chunky triangle shape.

11 Using a piping nozzle (tip), press a semi-circle into the pointed end of the shell. Add another four lines using the back of your knife to finish. Make about 10 of these shells and stick them around the cake with dabs of water.

12 To make the rocks, partially knead about 1 ounce (30 g) of both white and gray fondant together. Break off bits and roll into "rocks" and stick around the cake between the shells.

13 Lightly moisten the cake board and, using a teaspoon, spoon a little light brown sugar "sand" around the cake. Use the end of a soft paintbrush to coax it between the rocks and shells.

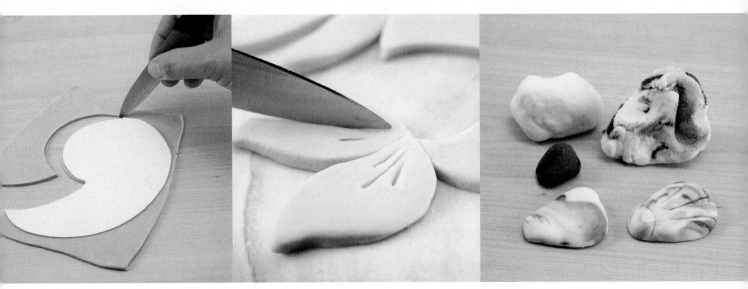

Dolphin Cupcakes

Use a few "shells," "rocks" and a light sprinkling of sand to make happy, seaside themed cupcakes.

Baby Shower Cupcakes

This is a fun idea that work very well for baby's first birthday or a christening or baby shower. You can almost hear the noisy chaotic racket from here!

To Make a Baby Shower Cupcake

Makes 12 cupcakes

Ingredients

14 oz (400 g) fondant. Use approximately
1 oz (30 g) flesh-colored fondant per
baby. (See page 27 for information
about creating different skin tones.)
2 quantities buttercream (see page 22)
Assorted food color gel for coloring hair
(brown, black, yellow)
Confectioners' sugar for rolling fondant
out on
Water, boiled and cooled, for sticking

Equipment

Pastry bag, optional (you do not need to
pipe onto your cupcakes, you could just
apply a large blob with a palette knife)
Large star tip—optional
Any small piping nozzle (tip)
Small soft paintbrush
Wooden spoon or ball tool
Small, sharp, non-serrated knife

> **TIP** Cover up any mistakes on your
> babies with dabs of buttercream. These
> guys are having fun so the messier
> the better!
>
> Use the tip of your paintbrush to
> lift and place the baby's tooth into the
> mouth. It's easier than trying to use
> your finger.

1 Make a head by rolling out about $1/2$ ounce (15 g) of flesh-colored fondant into a ball. Create a smiling mouth by holding a piping tip at an angle and pressing it into the fondant to leave a "U" shaped impression. Alternatively press it in upside down and make a sad mouth.

Other mouths can be made by poking the end of your paintbrush into the lower part of the head. A small hollow will give your baby a slightly shocked impression. Poke the brush in and pull it downward and suddenly he will look as though he's singing!

For a wailing baby, use the end of a wooden spoon or ball tool to create a large hollow in the lower part of his face. Stick a tiny white fondant square on the edge of the cavernous hole to look like baby's first tooth.

2 Make two tiny, flattened balls of white fondant for eyes (unless you're making a crying baby, in which case leave them out as the hands will cover the eyes) and stick them on the head with a light dab of water. Add a tiny flesh-colored ball of fondant for a nose.

3 Add two tiny flesh-colored ball shapes for ears and stick on the side of the baby's head. Poke the end of a paintbrush into each ear to both leave a small hollow and press the ears firmly into position.

4 Make two tiny, tapering sausage shapes for the arms. If your baby's hands are going to cover the face, stick them into position now, otherwise place them to one side for the moment.

5 Pipe or spread buttercream onto your cupcake. Gently place the head on top and place the hands in position.

6 Paint two tiny black food color dots on the eyes.

7 To make the hair, thinly roll out a little black, brown or yellow fondant. You can use your paintbrush as a miniature rolling pin to do this. Then press a few lines into the fondant with the back of your knife.

8 Holding your knife almost completely upright cut out a tiny leaf shape. Dab a little water on the baby's head and place the largest end of the leaf shape on the top of the head, lines facing downwards. Using your paintbrush, gently bend the rest of the hair backwards to produce a cute looking curl. Tweak into place using the tip of your paintbrush. Alternatively, create a small fondant rectangle and cut a fringe along one side. Stick it onto

the baby's head and splay the strands of the fringe using your paintbrush.

Another charming alternative is to leave the hair out altogether and pipe a blob of buttercream onto the top of the baby's head.

Baffled Biker Cake

This bemused biker, who has just been overtaken by a tortoise, has ridden into this book because "How do you make a standing up motorbike?" is one of the questions I'm most frequently asked. Here's how you do it...

Ingredients

8 in (20 cm) round cake
1 quantity buttercream (see page 22)
Confectioners' sugar for rolling out
   fondant on
Water, boiled and cooled, for sticking
1 lb 14 oz (850 g) green fondant
8 oz (250 g) gray fondant
8 oz (250 g) white fondant
7 oz (200 g) black fondant
1/3 oz (10 g) flesh-colored fondant
1 strand raw uncooked spaghetti
1 sheet edible wafer paper
Edible black writing pen
Black and green food color gels

Equipment

10 in (25 cm) round cake board
Carving knife
Palette knife
Rolling pin
Small, sharp, non-serrated knife
Medium and fine paintbrushes
Circle cutters—1 3/4 in (4.5 cm) and 3/4 in
   (2 cm)
Piping nozzle (tip), any design
Mudguard templates (see page 78)
Drinking straw
Scissors
Pastry bag (see page 79)

Baffled Biker Cupcakes

A tire is a simple decoration that would appeal to anyone who loves motorsports of any sort.

Cut out a thick black fondant disc and press a few lines around its edge with the back of a knife. Thinly roll out a little gray fondant and cut out a thin disc. Stick this onto the center and press a circular impression in the center using a piping tip. Smear a little chocolate buttercream "mud" over the top of the cupcake and place the tire on top.

To Make Your Baffled Biker Cake

1 Carve a few lumps out of the side of the cake and pile the lumps onto the back of the cake to add some height. Split and fill the middle with buttercream. Reassemble and place onto the board. Then put buttercream on the top and sides.

2 Knead and roll out 1 pound 12 ounces of (800 g) green fondant. Lift and cover the cake. Smooth into position and trim and neaten the base. Keep the excess green for the base.

3 Lightly moisten the exposed cake board. Roll the leftover green into a strip and lay and stick around the board. Trim and neaten the edges of the board.

4 Paint a little water up the sides and over the top of the cake to make it ready for the road. Knead and roll out 5 ounces (150 g) of gray fondant. Cut a strip about 17 inches x 3 inches (43 cm x 8 cm). Lay and stick across the center of the cake and board.

Trim and neaten and keep the excess gray. Partially knead the leftover gray into 7 ounces (200 g) of white fondant. Pull little bits off and stick around the base of the cake to look like rocks. Reserve a few to stick on the road later.

5 To make the bike, start with the wheels. Roll out about 4 ounces (120 g) of black-colored fondant no thinner than 1/3 inch (1 cm). Cut out a thick disc using the largest cutter. Re-roll the excess and cut out a second wheel.

6 Press a smaller circle into the center of each wheel using the smaller cutter. Thinly roll out about 1/8 ounce (5 g) of gray fondant and cut out two thin discs with a piping nozzle (tip). Stick one in the center of each wheel.

7 Roll 2 1/2 ounces (75 g) of gray fondant out to the same thickness as the black wheels. Cut out a square the same height as the wheels—approximately 1 1/2 inches (4 cm). Using the biggest circle cutter, take two "bites" out of the square. You should be left with a shape that looks a bit like an anvil. Stand this odd-shaped bit of fondant between the two upright wheels and stick all three together with a little water. It should stand steady. If it's too thin and wobbly, redo it and make the three components thicker.

8 To make the tread on the tires, press a few lines across the front and rear edges of the tires with the back of your knife. Make a small gray sausage for the exhaust and stick in place.

9 Thinly roll out about 2/3 ounce (20 g) of green fondant and cut out two tombstone shapes (use the template if you wish) for the mudguards. Stick one over each wheel.

10 Make a thick 1/3 ounce (10 g) of green carrot shape for the front of the bike. Flatten the front tip and stick in place on top of the front wheel.

11 Make a 1/8-ounce (5 g) thick, green triangular shape for the seat and stick on top of the bike.

12 Roll 1 ounce (30 g) of black fondant into a sausage about 6 1/2 inches (16 cm) long for the rider's legs. Slightly flatten each end and bend into "L" shapes for the feet. Arrange and stick the legs over the seat with the feet on the floor. Bend the rider's knees slightly. As well as being an essential part of the design, the legs provide additional stability for the bike.

13 Make a 1-ounce (30 g) white fondant cone shape for the body and stick on top of the legs. Insert a length of spaghetti for support, leaving about 3/4 inch (2 cm) protruding. Stick a white disc onto the front of the bike for its headlight.

14 Roll about 1/8 ounce (5 g) of gray fondant into a short sausage about 1 1/4 inches (3 cm) long for the handlebars. Stick on top of the bike in front of the rider's body.

15 Roll 1/2 ounce (15 g) of green fondant into a sausage about 6 inches (15 cm) long for the arms and cut in half. Using the rounded ends to form the shoulders, stick the two arms against the body, bending them at the elbows.

16 Make two black pea-sized ball-shapes for the hands and stick them on so they sit at both the end of the arms and against the ends of the handlebars. Make and stick two tiny flat

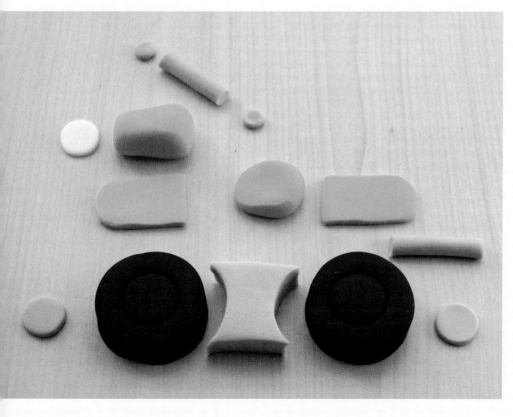

TIPS: You may find it easier to make both the rider and tortoise off the cake and stick them in place when they're finished. This also means you could make them a week or so before the cake is needed.

Use the rocks and grass to hide any problem areas on the cake.

Tortoise

gray discs on the side of each hand.

17 Roll ¹/₃ ounce (10 g) of green fondant into a ball for the helmet and stick onto the body.

18 Make a small flat flesh-colored oval and stick onto the front of the helmet. Add two tiny white ball shapes for eyes and a flesh ball for a nose.

19 To make the tortoise, partially knead ¹/₈ ounce (5 g) of black and ¹/₈ ounce (5 g) of green fondant together. Make into a thick disc for the shell. Make 4 tiny black sausage shapes for legs and stick under the shell. Make a fifth black sausage and stick onto the front of the shell. Bend the head forwards slightly. Press some circular impressions in the tortoise's shell with the end of a drinking straw and add two tiny white balls for eyes. Stick him onto the cake.

20 Draw two lines of "smoke" on the wafer paper with the edible writing pen and cut out. Insert one behind the bike's exhaust and the

other one behind the tortoise's rear leg.

21 To finish, stick the last few rocks in place next to the road. Color the leftover butter-cream green and place in a pastry bag. Close the bag and snip a tiny triangle off the end. Pipe grass along the edges of the road and amongst the rocks. Paint food color dots on the eyes and eyebrows on the biker.

Baffled Biker

Chocolate Butterfly Cupcakes

Made out of edible wafer paper (or rice paper) and dipped in chocolate, these decorations are incredibly easy to make but tremendously impressive. They could easily grace a sophisticated gateau, too. The paper is edible so it does not need to be removed before eating. The other element that enhances any cupcake is the wraps around the base.

Makes 12 butterflies

Ingredients
3–4 sheets edible wafer paper
4 oz (120 g) milk chocolate
4 oz (120 g) white chocolate
12 cupcake wrappers
1 quantity buttercream (see page 22)

Equipment
Pencil
Scissors
Small bowls for melting chocolate
2 teaspoons
Paper towels (your fingers will get sticky!)
Cereal box

TIP: You can speed up the time it takes the butterflies to set by placing them into the freezer or refrigerator for a short while.

If you want to add more decoration place a little melted chocolate in a piping bag and pipe a few swirls on the butterflies once they're set.

To Make Your Chocolate Butterfly Cupcakes

1 Fold a sheet of edible wafer paper in half and place the folded edge on the butterfly template.
2 Trace the butterfly wing outline and cut it out. Open up your butterfly and place it to one side.
3 Repeat, making as many edible wafer butterflies as you need and perhaps a couple of spares.

4 Make a mold for your butterflies to set on by cutting a section out of a cereal box that retains a right-angled edge.
5 Melt the milk and white chocolate in two separate bowls (see page 17 for details how to do this)
6 Take a butterfly and gently spoon a little of both chocolates onto one side of the butterfly.

7 Press the butterfly together to spread chocolate on the other side.
8 Open the butterfly up so its wings form a "V" shape and place onto the cereal box angle to set.
9 When they are ready, pipe or spoon some buttercream onto the top of your cupcakes and place a butterfly on top.

Chocolate Teddy Bear Cake

This design is probably one of the simplest and most forgiving cakes in this book because the messier the icing gets, the more loved and battered the teddy appears. The only drawback is that you will get very sticky when you're buttercreaming him (at least I did!).

Ingredients
2 pudding bowl cakes (see page 16)
2 quantities chocolate buttercream
   (see page 22)
4 small chocolate roll cakes
4 cupcakes
2/3 oz (20 g) black rolled fondant
2/3 oz (20 g) brown fondant
1/3 oz (10 g) white fondant
Chocolates discs/sweets to decorate
   the board (optional)

Equipment
12 in (30 cm) round cake board
1 pint heatproof pudding bowl
Sharp, non-serrated knife
Wood skewer or cake dowel
Palette knife
12 in (30 cm) ribbon
Scissors

TIP: Make sure the buttercream is nice and soft, if it's too hard it may tear the cake. Either beat it really well or soften for a few seconds in the microwave.

If you find the buttercream is picking up too many crumbs, cover the cake with a light coating of buttercream and place the cake into the fridge for about 15 minutes. The butter should harden and hold the crumbs in place allowing you to then cover it with a second coating of buttercream.

To Make Your Teddy Bear Cake

1 Turn one of the pudding bowl cakes upside down and split. Fill with buttercream if you wish. Reassemble and place towards the rear of the cake board.

2 Stick a cake dowel or wooden skewer into the body leaving about 3 inches (8 cm) protruding. If the second pudding bowl has risen into a dome while baking, slice a little off the top to level it. Also slice a little off one side to give the head a flat base to sit on

3 Carefully place the head—widest edge forwards—on top of the first cake. Use a hefty dab of buttercream to "glue" it into place.

4 Use the chocolate roll cakes to make the arms and legs. Use buttercream to stick them in position on the board and against the cake.

5 Cut a cupcake in half to make the ears and stick on the top of the head.

6 Stick another cupcake on the front of the face to form the bear's muzzle.

7 Place another two cupcakes at the end of the legs to form the feet.

8 Carefully coat the entire bear with chocolate buttercream and fluff it up slightly with a fork to make a furry effect.

9 To make the eyes, roll out a little brown and black fondant. Cut out two small brown discs using the larger piping nozzle (tip) or circle cutter. Make two slightly smaller black discs and stick on top.

10 Make two tiny, white fondant ball shapes. Flatten them and stick one on each eye to look like a highlight. Carefully stick the eyes into place.

11 Make a small black oval shape for the nose and stick onto the muzzle. Add a tiny white highlight as before.

12 Make a small black sausage shape and bend into an upside down "V" shape for the mouth. Place in position.

13 Add a bow, if desired, to finish and scatter some chocolate discs around the board. If you want the sweets to stay in place, spread some buttercream over the board first.

Baking Note: Although this design requires two bowl-shaped cakes you only need one bowl—bake one at a time.

If you don't have a bowl, bake a round cake instead and carve a little of the edges to make them rounded.

Chocolate Teddy Bear Cupcakes

Spread some chocolate buttercream over the top of the cupcake and rough it up a little with a fork to look like fur. Use two flat chocolate discs to make the ears and one to make the bear's muzzle. Make eyes and nose as shown above and add a flattened black fondant disc for a mouth.

Crazy Cars Cake

This is such a popular cake that you will find that every child that comes to the party will want to take a car home. This means you may find yourself having to make lots of cars—especially if it's a big party. The amounts given here are for 12–13 cars. As this could be a bit time consuming, I'd advise making the cars in advance. Make sure that they're no wider than 2 inches (5 cm) so that the ones that you place on the cake board will fit and not hang over the edges of the board.

Ingredients
8 in (20 cm) round cake
1 quantity buttercream (see page 22)
Confectioners' sugar for rolling out fondant on
Water, boiled and cooled, for sticking
2 lb 4 oz (1 kg) gray fondant
7 oz (200 g) red fondant
7 oz (200 g) blue fondant
7 oz (200 g) yellow fondant
7 oz (200 g) green fondant
5 oz (150 g) brown fondant
5 oz (150 g) flesh-colored fondant
5 oz (150 g) black fondant
Black and green food color gels

Equipment
12 in (30 cm) round cake board
Carving knife
Palette knife
Rolling pin
Small, sharp, non-serrated knife
Cake smoothers (optional)
Pastry brush
Fine and medium paintbrushes
Pastry bag—optional
Piping nozzle (tip) or drinking straw
Fork

Crazy Car Cupcakes

The little cars also look good driving across the top of a "muddy" chocolate butter-creamed cupcake.

TIPS: Personalize the license plates or paint the birthday child's age onto the license plates using black food gel.

A little black food color gel mixed into desiccated coconut makes very realistic looking "gravel" which you could use on the board if you prefer.

To Make Your Crazy Cars Cake

1 Slice the cake and fill with buttercream. Reassemble and place the cake in the center of the cake board. Spread buttercream around the sides and on top of the cake.

2 Knead 2 pounds 4 ounces (1 kg) of gray-colored fondant until pliable. Roll it out and lift and place over the cake. Smooth the top and sides and remove and keep the excess from around the base.

3 Using a pastry brush, moisten the exposed cake board around the cake with a little water. Use the leftover gray fondant to cover the cake board using the bandage method (see page 26)

4 Color the leftover buttercream green and, using either the tip of a knife or a pastry bag, carefully dab a circle of buttercream in the center of the cake and also around the top and bottom edges of the cake. Then "rough it up" with a fork to look like grass.

5 To make a car, mold 1 1/2 ounces (45 g) of red (or green or blue or yellow) fondant into a thick oval shape. Press on the front end lightly with your finger and squash it slightly.

6 Using your knife, make a cut halfway across the middle of the car. Then holding your knife flat, make a second horizontal cut at the back of the car that meets the first cut. Remove the resulting chunk of cut fondant. You should now be left with a shape that resembles a bedroom slipper!

7 Roll 1/8 ounce (5 g) of black fondant into a small sausage shape and slice it into five portions. Roll four of them into round, flattish wheels and stick them with light dabs of water around the car. Roll the fifth into a ball, flatten slightly and stick inside the car to make the steering wheel.

8 To make the driver, first choose the color of their clothing—red for example—and take a 1/3-ounce (10 g) lump of that color fondant. Roll three quarters of it into a ball for the body. Squash the ball slightly and stick inside the car. Keep the leftover bit of fondant for the arms.

9 Make a 1/3-ounce (10 g) ball of flesh-colored fondant for the head and stick it on top of the body and make a mouth. (See "Hair and Expressions" below)

10 Make two small flesh-colored balls for the hands and stick one on either side of the wheel. Also, make a tiny ball shape for the nose and stick onto the face.

11 Roll the leftover fondant from the body into a small sausage shape and cut it in half for the arms. Stick one on either side of the body.

12 Make two tiny, white ball shapes for the eyes. Flatten them and stick onto the face.

13 Make hair (see "Hair and Expressions" below) and add two tiny, flesh-colored balls for ears if necessary. Stick them on the sides of the head, and poke the end of a paintbrush into each ear to make a small hollow.

14 Make another four flat, white discs and stick one onto the center of each wheel.

15 Roll out and cut out a little white fondant and cut out a tiny rectangle and stick onto the front of the car for the number plate.

16 Make two tiny, yellow ball shapes for the headlights and stick onto the front of the car.

17 Paint black food color dots onto the eyes and stick your car in place on the cake with a light dab of water.

Hair and Expressions:

There are many ways you can make hair and expressions. Here are just a few simple suggestions:

1 **Happy face:** Make this by pressing a piping nozzle (tip) held at an angle into the fondant to leave a smiling "U" impression behind.

2 **Unhappy:** Press the piping tip upside down into the face.

3 **Umm-not-quite-sure face:** Hold your knife horizontal and press a line into the face.

4 **Shocked:** Poke the end of your paintbrush into the fondant to leave a small "o" impression.

5 **Long hair:** Roll out about 1/8-ounce (5 g) fondant and press lines down the length of it using the back of your knife. Cut out a rectangle. Dab a little water on the head and drape and lay the hair over the head. Using your knife, press a line across the head to make a center parting.

6 **Short hair:** Do the same as you did for long hair but with a smaller fondant rectangle. Use the end of a paintbrush to gently lift the front away from the face if you wish.

7 **Fringe/bangs:** Make a tiny, flat rectangle and make partial cuts along one long edge. Stick it onto the face above the eyes. Use the tip of your paintbrush to gently ease the bangs into position.

8 **Totally Unruly!:** Take a small piece of fondant and dip it in water. Squish it between your fingers to basically turn it into a sticky gooey mess! Place it on top of the head and tweak it into style with the end of your paintbrush.

Double Decker Cupcakes

Tiny cakes baked in mini cupcake cases or vol-au-vent cases make very pretty cake toppers when placed on top of ordinary cupcakes. They also make great miniature treats and would make a lovely gift presented in a small pretty box. If you have any children about you'll also find that miniature cakes are a huge hit at a tea party! See Lilly, Patch and Ginger on page 18 enjoying theirs.

Makes 12 cupcakes

Ingredients
12 regular sized cupcakes
12 miniature cupcakes
2 quantities buttercream (see page 22)
   (You need to be generous!)
Cake Sprinkles
Gumdrops or small sweets

Equipment
Pastry bag and large star
   nozzle (tip)

TIP: If you don't have a pastry bag, a generous dollop of buttercream applied with a spoon and palette knife will work just as well.

You could mix the flavors, using a chocolate cupcake with vanilla frosting on the bottom and vanilla cupcake with chocolate frosting on the top for example.

To Decorate Your Cupcakes

1 Pipe a buttercream swirl onto each of the large cupcakes.
2 Stand a mini cake securely on top of each main cake.

3 Pipe buttercream swirl on top of each mini cake. Starting from the outside again, pipe a swirl on top of each mini cake. The higher you go the more dramatic the effect.

4 Decorate the cakes with a few sprinkles and top each mini cake with a gumdrop or some other small sweet.

Flower Cupcakes

Each of these flower designs is fairly straightforward to make and the overall effect when they are displayed all together is stunning.

Roses
(These are per rose so multiply amounts by the number of roses you'll need)

Ingredients
2/3 oz (20 g) pink fondant
1/2 oz (15 g) green fondant
Confectioners' sugar for rolling out fondant on
Water, boiled and cooled, for sticking

Equipment
Rolling pin
Small, sharp, non-serrated knife
Paintbrush
Leaf templates (page 78)

Five-Petal Flowers
(These are per flower so multiply amounts by the number of flowers you need)

Ingredients
2/3 oz (20 g) pink fondant
1 oz (30 g) green fondant
1/8 oz (5 g) yellow fondant
Confectioners' sugar for rolling out fondant on
Water, boiled and cooled, for sticking

Equipment
Rolling pin
5-petal flower cutter (optional—see "TIP" on page 47)
Small, sharp, non-serrated knife
Paintbrush
Small circle cutter or piping nozzle (tip)

Edible Paper Flowers
If you cannot find pink wafer paper (also called edible rice paper), you could either just make white edible flowers or dust some wafer paper with some edible pink dusting powder, which you can find in cake decorating equipment stores. If you're using edible paper, then keep it well away from any birthday candles!

Ingredients
1 sheet pink wafer paper per flower
1 sheet white wafer paper per flower

Equipment
Pencil
Scissors
Heart template (page 78)

Edible Paper Flowers

How to Make Rose Cupcakes

1 Roll ²/3 ounce (20 g) of pink fondant into a sausage about 6 inches (15 cm) long.

2 Press along one long edge of the sausage with the pads of your fingers to flatten it into a sloping strip with one long thick edge and one long thin one. Alternatively roll along one edge with your rolling pin.

3 Slide your knife under the strip to make sure it's not stuck to your work surface.

4 Paint a light line of water along the thick edge of the strip.

5 Carefully start to roll the strip up like a loose bandage. The thick part of the strip should form the base.

6 Lightly squeeze the base together. This should automatically open the rose up. Using your paintbrush, tweak the edges of the petals into an attractive arrangement.

7 Slice a little off the bottom of the rose to make a flat base for it to sit on. Put to one side while you make the rest of your roses.

8 When ready, pipe buttercream onto the cupcakes and place a rose and a leaf in the center.

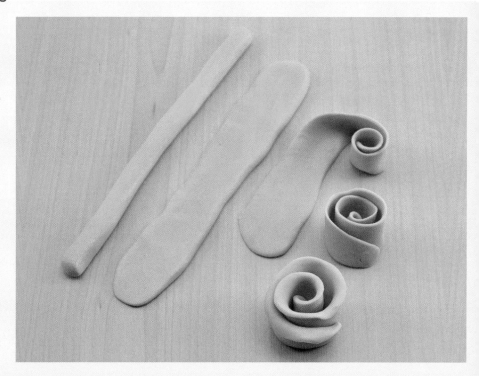

How to Make Five-Petal Flower Cupcakes

1 Begin with the leaves so that they have a bit of time to dry out and harden. You will need three leaves per flower. It would also be wise to make a few spares in case of breakages.

2 To make the flowers, thinly roll out about 2 ounces (60 g) of pink fondant and cut out two or three flower shapes using the flower cutter. If you have time, allow them to harden for a couple of hours. Scrunch up and re-use the pink fondant to make more flowers.

3 Roll out the yellow fondant and using a piping nozzle (tip) or small circle cutter, cut out the required number of yellow discs for the flower centers. Stick a yellow disc in the middle of each pink flower with a dab of water.

4 When you are ready to assemble the cupcakes, pipe or spread buttercream onto the top of each cake. Gently place a flower in the center. Carefully insert two or three leaves into the buttercream beneath the edges of the flower.

How to Make Leaves for Cupcakes

1 Thinly roll out about 2 ounces (60 g) of green fondant. Holding your knife almost upright, cut out three or four simple leaf shapes.
2 Press a line into the center of one leaf with the back of your knife and three angled lines.
3 Stick the leaf immediately with a dab of water onto the cake against the side of the rose. Repeat on the rest of the roses.

TIP: The leaves on these cakes are colored using a food color gel in a shade called "gooseberry." If you don't have this color, either use another shade of green or knead some yellow and brown food color into some regular green fondant.

If you like the look of the five petal flowers but don't possess a cutter, simply use a piping nozzle (tip) or something similar to cut out five pink discs per flower. Alternatively, you could just make five pink ball shapes and flatten them.

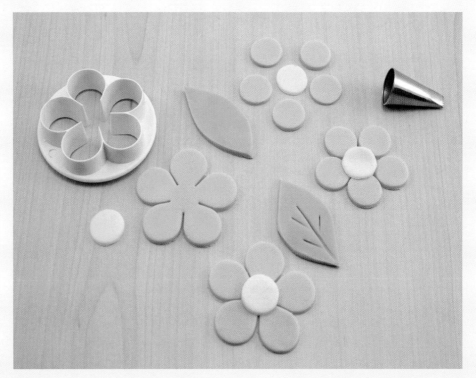

How to Make Edible Paper Flowers

1 Fold a strip of edible wafer paper in half. Place the folded edge against the straight edge of the heart template.
2 Using a sharp pencil trace over the template.
3 Cutting just inside the lines, cut around the outline and open up the heart-shaped petal. Make three pink and three white petals per flower.
4 When ready to use, pipe buttercream onto the top of the cake. Arrange the petals in alternative colors in a flower shape on top of the cake.
5 Pipe a small buttercream star in the center of each flower to finish.

Football Player Cake

It's worth mastering how to make a sitting person as it is a really useful and easy way to place a full-length character on a cake.

Ingredients
7 in (18 cm) round sponge cake
1 quantity buttercream (see page 22)
Confectioners' sugar for rolling out the fondant on
Water, boiled and cooled for sticking
1 lb 8 oz (700 g) white fondant
3 oz (90 g) blue fondant
1 oz (30 g) brown fondant

1 strand raw, uncooked spaghetti
Black and green food color gels

Equipment
10 in (25 cm) round cake board
Carving knife
Palette knife
Rolling pin
Cake smoother (optional)

Small, sharp, non-serrated knife
Fine and medium paintbrushes
2¹/4 in (5.5 cm) circle cutter or lid or template
24 in (61 cm) ribbon
Scissors
Clear sticky tape

Football Cupcakes

Cover the top of the cupcake with green buttercream. Rough it up with a fork to make it look like grass. Make a football (Step 7) and place it on the cake.

Making the Football Player

1 Level the top of your cake and turn it upside down. Slice the cake into two or three layers and fill with buttercream.

2 Place the cake in the center of the cake board and spread a thin coating of buttercream around the sides and top.

3 Dust your work surface with confectioners' sugar and knead and roll out 1 pound 5 ounces (600 g) of white fondant. Lift the fondant and cover the cake. Smooth the top and sides and trim and neaten around the base.

4 Roll 1 1/2 ounces (45 g) of white fondant into a sausage about 5 inches (12 cm) long for the player's legs. Bend it into a "U" shape and stick on top of the cake

5 Roll 2 ounces (60 g) into a tapering oval shape for his body. Stick onto the body with the widest part forming his shoulders. Stick a bit of spaghetti inside the body to provide

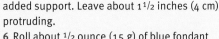

added support. Leave about 1 1/2 inches (4 cm) protruding.

6 Roll about 1/2 ounce (15 g) of blue fondant into a sausage about 3 1/8-inch (8 cm) long for his socks. Cut the sausage in half and stick one on the end of each leg.

7 To make the ball, roll 1/8 ounce (5 g) of brown fondant into an oval then pinch the ends to make an authentic football shape. Press a line down its length using your knife and 8 or 9 tiny lines across it using just the tip of your knife. Place to one side for a moment.

8 Make two 1/3-ounce (10 g) tapering white sausage shapes for the arms. They should be thicker at one end. Stick them onto the body with the thickest end forming his shoulders.

9 Make two small, brown ball shapes for the hands and flatten slightly. Stick the ball in position on his chest and stick the hands on top as though he's holding it.

10 Roll 1/2 ounce (15 g) of brown fondant into a ball shape for his head and stick on top of his body.

11 Add two tiny, flattened, white ball shapes for his eyes and a small ball of brown for his nose.

12 To make the helmet, thinly roll out about 2/3 ounce (20 g) of white fondant and using a circle cutter, lid or template cut out a disc.

13 Cut a strip off the disc. Lightly moisten the player's head with a little water and lay the largest section of the disc over the player's head. The flat cut edge should form the front of the helmet.

14 To make the face guard press a few vertical lines across the smaller bit of the disc with the back of your knife. Then press one line horizontally across it. Stick it across the lower part of his face.

15 Stick one tiny flattened blue discs on each side of his helmet and paint two black dots on his eyes.

16 Make two 1/3-ounce (5 g) white oval shapes for his feet and stick one onto the end of each leg.

17 To finish, paint a little watered down green food coloring around the figure on top of the cake and stand ribbon around the base. Secure it at the back with a little sticky tape.

TIP: As with the Soccer Cake, alter the colors, skin tones and any other details to match those of your favorite team.

Instead of covering the cake with fondant you could cover it with green buttercream "grass" instead. Make the figure off the cake first and then place him in position on the cake once he's ready.

Goofy Golfers Cake

Standing a covered cake board at the back of a cake is an easy way to provide support for a standing character and will add a different dimension to your cakes—literally!

Ingredients

8 in (20 cm) round cake
1 quantity buttercream (see page 22)
Confectioners' sugar for rolling out fondant on
Water, boiled and cooled, for sticking
6 oz (175 g) pale blue fondant
1 lb 15 oz (900 g) green fondant
1 oz (30 g) black fondant
8 oz (250 g) white fondant
1 oz (30 g) pink fondant
2 oz (60 g) flesh-colored fondant
1/3 oz (10 g) gray fondant
Black food color gel
3 teaspoons soft, light brown sugar

Equipment

10 in (25 cm) round cake board
8 in (20 cm) round THIN cake card
Medium and fine paintbrushes
Rolling pin
Carving knife
Palette knife
Cake smoothers (optional)
Small, sharp, non-serrated knife
1 wooden skewer
Piping nozzle (tip), any design, or a drinking straw
Teaspoon

1 Begin by covering the thin cake board that will form the background. Moisten the entire board with a little water. Thinly roll out about 3 1/2 ounces (100 g) of pale blue fondant and lay it over the top third of the board. Cut a wavy line along the edge that will form the horizon and remove and keep the excess.

2 Thinly roll out about 3 1/2 ounces (100 g) of green fondant and cover the lower portion of the board. Trim away the excess from around the edges. Lay it flat and, ideally, allow to harden for a couple of hours.

3 Before covering the cake, slice a section off the back to form a flat edge for the covered board to stand against. Cut a small hollow out of the top of the cake for the bunker.

4 Slice, fill and coat the cake with buttercream. Then cover it using 1 pound 12 ounces (800 g) of green fondant keeping the excess. The flat edge should be at the back.

5 Moisten the exposed cake board around the cake. Use the leftover green fondant to cover the board stopping and starting parallel to the flat back edge. Use the bandage method to do this (see page 26). You do not have to cover the area right at the back.

6 Partially knead about 2/3 ounce (20 g) of black fondant into 7 ounces (200 g) of white to get a marbled-effect. Place about 3 ounces (90 g) of this marbled fondant to one side. Pull the rest into bits and roll into small rocks. Stick them around the base of the cake.

7 Moisten the flat back edge of the cake and stand the covered background board against it. Press it gently into place and use a few large "rocks" behind it to hold it in place. Add another line of rocks along the top edge of the cake against the vertical board.

Golfing Cupcakes

Spread a little apricot jam over the top of the cupcake. Roll out and cut out a disc of green fondant. Place the disc on top of the cupcake. Roll a little brown fondant into a thin string for the golf club handle. Roll a little gray into a small "L" shape and press a few lines into the base with the back of your knife. Place the handle and base together and lay and stick on top of the cake. Paint the handle with black food color. Make a tiny white ball and poke a few holes in it using the tip of a toothpick.

To Make Your Golfers

1 To make the lady golfer, start with her feet. Make two $1/8$-ounce (5 g) pink fondant ovals for her shoes and stick on top of the cake against the backboard.

2 Roll $1/8$ ounce (5 g) of white fondant into an oval for her socks. Cut it in two and stick one half on top of each shoe.

3 Make two thin strings of flesh-colored fondant and stick against the board and on top of the socks. For her shorts, thinly roll out $1/3$ ounce (10 g) of pink fondant and cut out a trapezium shape. Make a partial cut up the center and stick over the legs.

4 Make a $1/8$-ounce (5 g) white oval and flatten it for her torso. Stick it on top of the shorts. Make two thin white strings for her arms. Bend them slightly at the elbows and stick against her body.

5 Make a small, flesh-colored oval shape for the head. Flatten it and stick on top of her body. Poke a hollow with the end of a paintbrush to make a mouth. Add two tiny white ball shapes for eyes and a flesh ball for her nose.

6 Make and stick a thin pink strip around the top of her head. Add a tiny, pink semi-circle for a visor. Dip about $1/8$ ounce (5 g) of black fondant into some water and rub it between your fingers until it's really sticky. Pull bits off and use this to make her hair.

TIP: Hide any unsightly bits of cake icing with a rock!

For a simpler version of this design, leave the backboard and standing golfer out and just make a round cake and un-happy golfer in the bunker. He'll still make people smile!

7 Stand a cut length of wood skewer between the end of one arm and the top of the cake. Make two flesh-colored ball shapes for hands and flatten. Stick them in place with one over the top of the skewer.

8 Make a tiny gray oval for the head of the club. Press a few lines into it with the back of a knife. Stick on top of the cake at the other end of the skewer.

9 Paint two black dots on the eyes and a little black on the top of the skewer to look like the handle.

10 For the man, roll 1 1/2 ounces (45 g) of blue fondant into an oval for his body and stick in-side the hollow. Make a 1/2-ounce (15 g) flesh-colored ball for the head and stick on top of the body. Press a piping nozzle (tip) or straw into his face to make a glum-looking mouth.

11 Add eyes and a nose as before. Stick an-other two flesh-colored ball shapes on the sides of his head for ears and poke the end of a paintbrush into each one.

12 Flatten a small ball of blue fondant into a thin disc for his cap. Tweak the front upwards to form a peak and stick on top of his head.

13 Roll 1/2 ounce (15 g) blue fondant into a sausage for his arms and cut in half. Bend them and stick in place. Stick a small ball of flesh-colored fondant between the ends of the arms for his hands and add a golf club and dots on the eyes as before.

14 To finish, spoon a little brown sugar into the bunker and add a tiny white fon-dant ball.

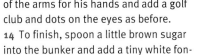

Happy Hamsters Cake

These busy little fellows can't wait for the party to start. Make sure you make enough so everyone can take one home!

Ingredients
8 in (20 cm) square sponge cake
2 quantities chocolate buttercream
  (see page 22)
2 packs long, thin chocolate cookies
  or similar
Confectioners' sugar for rolling out
  fondant on
Water, boiled and cooled, for sticking
12 oz (350 g) black fondant
1 lb (450 g) brown fondant
1 lb 4 oz (550 g) white fondant
1 oz (30 g) pink fondant
2 oz (60 g) orange fondant
1 oz (30 g) green fondant

Equipment
12 in (30 cm) square cake board
Carving knife
Palette knife
Rolling pin
2¹/₂ in (6.5 cm) circle cutter (optional)
Tiny ¹/₂ in (12 mm) circle cutter,
  piping nozzle (tip) or lid
Small, sharp, non-serrated knife
Toothpick
Small paintbrush
Cheese grater

TIP: To stop crumbs from getting everywhere, spread a thin coat of soft buttercream over the outside of the cake. Place the cake into the refrigerator for at least 20 minutes or until the buttercream has hardened. Remove from the refrigerator and spread a thick coating over the cake.
  Use your paintbrush as a small rolling pin for flattening the tiny pieces of fondant for the ears.

Happy Hamster Cupcakes

Place a hamster on top of a cupcake and sprinkle some "sawdust" around him.

To Make Your Happy Hamsters Cake

1 Level the top of the cake and lay it flat. Slice the tip off of two diagonally opposite corners. Then slice the cake diagonally in half to make two triangles. Cut one of the triangles in half again. Discard or eat the two tiny pointed ends.

2 Stand the largest section of cake upright. The longest edge of the triangle should form the base. Stand it diagonally on the board. Place the two remaining sections in place against it. It should look like a cross when viewed from above. Level and neaten the top platform to make it flat.

3 Spread buttercream over the outside of the cake (see "Tip") and press the chocolate cookies into the icing to make the ramps.

4 To make a tunnel, either flatten a 2/3 ounce, (20 g) ball of black fondant into a disc, or roll it out flat and cut out a circle using the large cutter. Make two and press into the side of the cake.

5 Construct two hamsters at a time. Make two 1-ounce (30 g) fondant oval shapes, one white and one brown.

6 Slice both ovals into three and remove the two middle strips. Reassemble the ovals with the white middle strip in the center of the two brown ends and the brown strip in the middle of the white. Use dabs of water to stick the fondant together.

7 Pinch a small tail into the rear of each hamster and make a mouth by holding your knife upright and pressing a small line into the front of the face.

8 Thinly roll out a little pink and brown fondant for the ears. Dab a little water on the brown and place the pink on top. Cut out two discs using either a small circle cutter, piping nozzle (tip) or lid.

9 Cut both discs in half and with the pink on the inside, fold each half over to form an ear. Stick one ear on either side of head.

10 Make two tiny pink fondant balls for noses and stick one on each hamster.

11 Place a little black food coloring in a dish and dip the tip of a toothpick into it. Give each hamster's face two dots for eyes. Repeat, making as many hamsters as you need and arrange them on the board and cake. Dab a little water on the base of the hamsters climbing up the ramps to hold them in place. Just make heads and bodies for the hamsters coming out of the tunnels.

12 To make the standing up hamster, roll about 1 ounce (30 g) of brown fondant into a tapering oval shape. Stand upright with the thickest part forming the base. Bend the head forward slightly.

13 Add ears, eyes, nose and mouth as before and make two tiny brown sausage shapes for

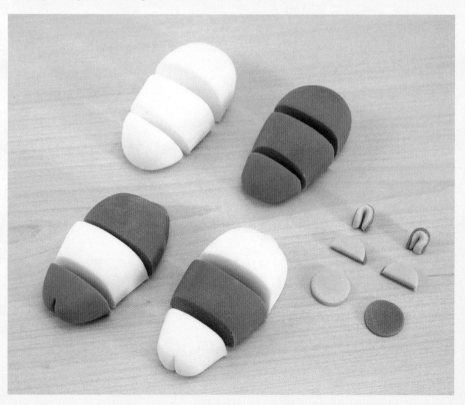

paws. Bend the ends of the paws forward and stick onto the front of the hamster.

14 To make a carrot, roll out about ²/₃ ounce (20 g) of orange-colored fondant into a carrot shape. Press a few lines across the top using the back of your knife. Make a tiny, green fondant carrot shape for the leaves and cut into a fringe. Fan the leaves slightly. Stick onto the end of the carrot and place onto the cake.

15 To make the saw dust, partially knead about 3¹/₂ ounces (100 g) of brown fondant and 7 ounces (200 g) of white together. Stop before it becomes a solid color.

16 Lightly dab water around the exposed cake board. Grate the fondant using the cheese grater and carefully spoon over the cake board.

Ice Cream Cone Cupcakes

They may not look like it but these really are cakes. The cake mixture has been baked inside the cones and the "ice cream" is a generous dollop of buttercream, although you could top them with a scoop of real ice cream if you prefer. To make the pink-colored "ice cream" I simply stirred a teaspoonful of jam into the vanilla buttercream.

Ingredients for making 10 cakes
10 flat-bottomed ice cream cones
2 egg quantity of Madeira cake mixture
   (see page 14)
1 quantity buttercream (see page 22)
Chocolate, sprinkles, jam, chocolate sticks,
   etc. for decoration

Equipment
Tin foil
Spoon
Baking tray
Palette knife

TIP: Experiment with different flavors. For example, stir a little lemon zest in to the cake mixture before baking.

Stir a handful of chocolate chips into the buttercream for chocolate chip ice cream cupcakes with a bit of texture!

To Make Your Ice Cream Cone Cupcakes

1 Wrap a little tin foil around the outside of each empty cone. This will stop it from burning in the oven.
2 Mix up the cake mixture and pre-heat your oven to 300° F (150° C).
3 Spoon the cake mixture into the cones fill-ing the cones about two-thirds full. Stand the cones on the baking tray and carefully place into the oven.
4 Cook for about 25 minutes until golden and springy to the touch. If you're unsure, insert a skewer into the center of one of the cakes. If it comes out clean, the cake is cooked.
5 Remove the tin foil and allow the cakes to cool.
6 Once cooled, spread buttercream onto the top of each cake and finish with some sprin-kles, melted chocolate, or anything else.

Cute Kitty Cupcakes

Cats always like to find a comfortable place to rest and what could be a sweeter place than a nice squishy cupcake? There are three styles of cats: sitting, lying sideways, and lying facing forwards. There are three styles of faces: sleeping, normal and with eyelids. By mixing them up, all your cats will appear to look totally different.

Makes 9 cupcakes

Ingredients
9 cupcakes
2 quantities buttercream (see page 22)
Confectioners' sugar for rolling out
    fondant on
Water, boiled and cooled, for sticking
1 lb (450 g) brown fondant
1½ oz (45 g) white fondant
½ oz (15 g) pink fondant
Black food color gel

Equipment
Fine and medium paintbrushes
Piping nozzle (tip), circle cutter or small
    lid
Small, sharp, non-serrated knife
Toothpick
Drinking straw
Pastry bag & large star nozzle (tip)
    (decorator's bag & star tip)—optional

TIP: You can vary the breed of cats by using different colored fondants or painting food color stripes on them.
    If you don't like using piping, put a dollop of green-colored buttercream green on each cake and sit your kittens on "grass" instead.

To Make Your Cute Kitty Cupcakes

Sitting Kitty

1 Make a 1-ounce (30 g) brown fondant oval shape for the body. Flatten the base and top slightly so it sits upright securely.

2 Holding your knife upright, press three lines into the base of the body for its legs.

3 Make a 1/2-ounce (15 g) ball for the head and a tiny brown fondant string shape for the tail. Stick both in place with tiny dabs of water.

4 Make two tiny, white fondant ball shapes for the eyes. Flatten them and stick onto the face.

5 Make a tiny, pink fondant oval for the tongue and stick onto the lower part of the face.

6 To make the cat's muzzle, make another two tiny, white ball shapes and flatten them. Stick them over the tongue.

7 Using the tip of a toothpick press three tiny dots into each side of the cat's muzzle.

8 For the ears, roll out a tiny bit of pink fon-dant and cut out a tiny, pink square shape. Roll out a little brown fondant and stick the pink square on top. Carefully cut around the pink square ensuring that the brown is slightly bigger than the pink.

9 Cut the square in half diagonally to form two triangular ears. Stick the ears on the side of the head.

10 To finish, dip the tip of a toothpick into some black food coloring and use it to make two dots on the eyes.

Sideways Kitty

1 Make a 1-ounce (30 g) brown fondant oval shape for the body. Using a small circle cutter or lid, press a circular indent into the rear of the kitten's body.

2 Make a small fondant tail and a head as be-fore and stick onto the body.

Forward Facing Kitty

1 Make a 1-ounce (30 g) oval for the body and flatten the front of the cat's body slightly.

2 Make a head as before and stick on the front of the body.

3 Make a tiny fondant string for the tail and stick on the rear of the cat allowing the tail to stand upright. Bend it into a bit of a curve.

Facial Variations

1 For closed eyes, use a drinking straw held at an angle to press two "U" shapes into the fondant.

2 For eyelids, make a tiny ball of brown fon-dant. Flatten it and cut it in half and stick one half at an angle over each eye.

3 To assemble the cupcakes, pipe buttercream onto the top of each cupcake and place a cat on top.

Makeup Bag Cake

Although my bottles and brushes are very simple, you could add a terrific personal touch by making fondant copies of the recipient's favorite makeup.

Ingredients
8 in (20 cm) round sponge cake
1 quantity buttercream (see page 22 for recipe)
Confectioners' sugar for rolling out fondant on
Water, boiled and cooled, for sticking
2 lb 11 oz (1.2 kg) white fondant
8 oz (250 g) pink fondant
2 oz (60 g) purple fondant
1¹/₂ oz (45 g) black fondant
7 oz (200 g) gray fondant

Equipment
12 in (30 cm) round cake board
Carving knife
Palette knife
Rolling pin
Cake smoothers (optional)
Small, sharp, non-serrated knife
1 in (2.5 cm) circle cutter or lid (see "TIP")
Piping nozzle (tip) of any design
Small soft paintbrush
Pastry brush

TIP: If you don't have circle cutters, make balls of fondant and squash them to make flat disc shapes instead.

Make the cosmetics before you cover the board otherwise the fondant will have started to dry out and could crack when you're placing them into position.

Makeup Bag Cupcakes

Create your makeup items as shown above. Spread a little apricot jam onto the top of each cupcake and thinly roll out a little white fondant. Cut out a disc and place it on top of the cupcake allowing it to fall into folds. Alternatively, pipe a buttercream swirl instead. Then place your makeup item on top.

To Make Your Makeup Bag Cake

1 Create the small jars by making two 1-ounce (30 g) white fondant ball shapes. Thickly roll out ¹/₈ ounce (5 g) of both purple and pink fondant and using the circle cutter, cut out two thick discs for the lids. Stick the lids on top of their white bases.

2 For the nail varnish, make a ¹/₂-ounce (15 g) pink fondant carrot shape. Slice a little off the top and bottom and stand upright. Make a second ¹/₈-ounce (5 g) gray carrot shape for the lid and again slice off the two ends. Stick the lid on top of the base with a light dab of water.

3 Thinly roll out a little white fondant and cut out a flat disc shape for the label using a piping nozzle (tip) as a cutter. Stick on the front of the bottle. Repeat making a second bottle but using ¹/₂ ounce (15 g) of purple fondant for the base.

4 To make the compact, make two ¹/₃-ounce (10 g) gray fondant balls and flatten into thick discs. Thinly roll out ¹/₈ ounce (5 g) of purple and pink fondant and cut out two discs with the circle cutter and stick on top of the gray.

5 For the applicator, make two tiny white balls and a thin white fondant stick. Flatten the balls and stick one on either end of the stick.

6 For the lipsticks, make three ¹/₃-ounce (10 g) chunky sausage shapes—one pink, one purple and one gray. Slice the rounded ends off each sausage and cut the gray sausage in half. Make two ¹/₃-ounce (10 g) pink sausage shapes and slice one rounded end off each. Cut a slope into the other end. Assemble and stick the lipsticks together.

7 To make the blusher brush make a ¹/₃-ounce (10 g) pink sausage about 2 inches (5 cm) long for the handle. Slice and discard the rounded ends. Roll about ¹/₈ ounce (5 g) of gray into an oval and slice off the rounded ends. Press a few lines across the gray using the back of your knife.

8 Roll ¹/₃ ounce (10 g) of black fondant into a carrot shape. Press lines down its length and

slice off the two rounded ends. Stick the brush, handle and gray centerpiece together.

9 Cut the cake to shape by slicing a 1-inch (2.5 cm) strip off the back of the cake.

10 Cut a slope into the front of the cake and split and fill the cake with jam or buttercream.

11 Reassemble the cake and place towards the rear of the cake board. Coat the outside of the cake with buttercream.

12 Dust your work surface with confectioners' sugar and knead and roll out 1 pound 10 ounces (750 g) of white fondant. Cover the cake and smooth the top and sides. Trim and neaten around the base

13 Thinly roll out about 1 ounce (30 g) of pink fondant. Cut out 4 flat discs using the circle cutter. Stick with light dabs of water onto the top of the bag. Repeat using 1 ounce (30 g) of black, purple and gray fondant.

14 Knead 12 ounces (350 g) of white fondant with the rest of the pink (you should have about 5 ounces/150 g of pink left) together to make a light pink shade. Keep kneading until all the streaks are gone.

15 Moisten the exposed board around the cake by lightly painting it with water using a pastry brush.

16 Roll out the light pink fondant to a ¹/₄ inch (5 mm) thickness. Arrange the fondant around the cake on the board, allowing it to fall into waves and folds. Gently press it down at the

edges of the board (a cake smoother is useful for doing this) and trim and neaten the edges. Move onto the next step quickly as the bag's openings need to sit on top of the pink base covering. If you let the pink firm up, your clasps won't lay flat.

17 Make two 1¹/₂ ounces (45 g) of gray fondant sausage shapes about 8 inches (20 cm) long for the bag's opening. Lay and stick them on top of each other at the front of the bag, gently pressing them into the fondant so they lay flat.

18 Make two ¹/₈-ounce (5 g) gray balls and flatten into discs. Stick one at each end of the opening and press a circle and small hollow in the center of each one using a piping nozzle (tip) and the end of a paintbrush.

19 Make two ¹/₈-ounce (5 g) gray carrot shapes for the clasp and stick on top of each other facing in different directions.

Merry Mermaid Cake

This design involves a bit of piping for the hair. It is easy to do, but if you're unsure or worried, apply a fancy buttercream hairdo with a small knife or use thin strips of fondant instead.

Ingredients
8 in (20 cm) round sponge cake
2 quantities buttercream (see page 22)
Confectioners' sugar for rolling out
    fondant on
Water, boiled and cooled, for sticking
1 oz (30 g) black fondant
1 lb 10 oz (750 g) white fondant
3 oz (90 g) flesh-colored fondant
10 oz (300 g) green fondant
1 oz (30 g) yellow fondant
Black and blue food color gels

Equipment
12 in (30 cm) round cake board
Carving knife
Palette knife
Rolling pin
Small, sharp, non-serrated knife
Medium and fine paintbrushes
Pastry bag (see page 79)
No. 4 piping nozzle (tip)—this is optional
    see the "TIP" for an alternative
Drinking straw (optional—you won't need
    this if you have a piping nozzle [tip])
Bowl for mixing leftover fondant

TIPS: If you don't have a piping tip make up a greaseproof bag and place the icing inside it. Close the bag and snip a tiny triangle off the end and pipe the hair.

Use a paintbrush to ease the sea into awkward areas around the rocks.

Mermaid Cupcakes

Spread a little apricot jam over the top of the cupcake. Partially knead a little blue and white fondant together to get a marbled effect then roll it out. Cut out a disc shape and place on top of the cupcake. Make a $1/3$-ounce (10 g) green fondant triangle for her tail and stick on top of the cake. Press a few scales into the tail using a drinking straw. Make two thick leaf shapes and press a few lines into each one and stick on the end of the tail. Pipe or apply some plain buttercream around the base of the tail then use a damp paintbrush to gently stroke it and pull it down towards the top of the cupcake which will make it look like a splash.

To Make Your Merry Mermaid Cake

1 Carve the cake into a rock shape by cutting a few chunks out of the sides. Use the cut out pieces to put on the top of the cake to provide extra height.

2 Slice the cake and fill with buttercream. Reassemble and stand the cake towards the rear of the cake board. Spread a thin coating of buttercream around the top and sides.

3 To cover the cake so it looks like a rock, break 1 ounce (30 g) of black fondant into four or five pieces. Shape one into a triangle for the shark's fin and place to one side. Wrap and keep a small bit of white fondant (about 1/8 ounce/5 g) to use for the eyes later. Partially knead the rest of the white and the rest of the black together. You should see a marbled-effect start to happen. Stop kneading before it becomes a solid matte color.

4 Roll out the marbled gray fondant to a thickness no thinner than 1/3 inch (1 cm). Lift it over the cake and smooth into place. Trim around the base and keep the excess.

5 Roll the leftover gray fondant into little rock shapes. Stick them around the base and top of the cake with light dabs of water.

6 To make the mermaid's body, roll 1 ounce (30 g) of flesh-colored fondant into a flattish oval shape and stick on top of the cake. Lean it against a rock to provide support.

7 Make a 1-ounce (30 g) flesh-colored ball for her head and stick on top of the body. Make a tiny ball for the nose and stick on the face.

8 For the arms, roll 1/2-ounce (15 g) flesh colored fondant into a sausage about 7 inches (18 cm) long and cut it in half. Squash the rounded end of each half section to make hands and arrange and stick the arms in position.

9 To make the tail, roll 3 ounces (90 g) of green fondant into a tapering triangle about 9 inches (22 cm) long. Arrange and stick it in place on the cake. Make the scales on the tail by press-ing a piping nozzle (tip) or drinking straw held at an angle into the still soft fondant.

10 To make the ends of the tail, roll out 2/3 ounce (20 g) of green fondant to a thickness of about 1/3 inch (1 cm). Cut out two simple leaf shapes. Press three lines into each one using the back of your knife. Stick the tail ends into position.

11 Make the octopus by rolling out 2 ounces (60 g) of green fondant into a ball and flattening it slightly. Stick it behind the cake as though it's peering over it.

12 To make the octopus' legs, roll 1 ounce (30 g) of green fondant into a sausage about 11 inches (27 cm) long. Cut it in half and arrange and stick the legs into position. Repeat this another three times. (There's no point in doing less than eight—there will always be at least one pedantic kid at the party who will count them to check if it has the right amount of legs!)

13 To make the crab, roll 2/3 ounce (20 g) of yellow fondant into a ball. Flatten it slightly and stick onto the cake or a rock.

14 Make two 1/8-ounce (5 g) yellow balls for the claws and again flatten them slightly. Cut halfway across each claw and open the claws up. Stick them on the front of the crab.

15 Make two round white balls for eyes and stick on the front of the crab. Make another two white fondant balls for eyes for the octopus and two tiny ones for the mermaid. Squash both sets of eyes to flatten them and stick them in place.

16 For the octopus eyelids, make a small green fondant ball and flatten it. Cut it in half and stick one half over each eye at a slight angle.

17 Using a fine paint brush and black food coloring, paint dots on the eyes of the crab and octopus and a sort of thick "U" shape on the mermaid's eyes. Also give the mermaid some eyelashes and a mouth.

18 Place about a tablespoon of vanilla buttercream in a pastry bag with a Number 4 nozzle (tip) fitted. Close the bag and pipe strands of hair over the rock and mermaid's body.

19 Place all leftover buttercream in a bowl and add a dab of blue food color. Partially stir the color into the icing but stop before it becomes a solid color. Swirl and smear it around the exposed cake board. Take the shark fin you made earlier and stand it in the "Water."

Pony Rider Cake

Although she may look like a complicated model, the rider is made out of simple shapes that are easy to create. If you want to allow yourself time to put her together, make her a week or so in advance and pop the figure onto the cake when you're ready.

Ingredients
7 in (18 cm) round sponge cake
1 quantity buttercream (see page 22)
Confectioners' sugar for rolling out fondant on
Water, boiled and cooled, for sticking
7 oz (200g) brown fondant
1/8 oz (5 g) orange fondant
1 lb 14 oz (850 g) white fondant
1/2 oz (15 g) black fondant
1 oz (30 g) red fondant
1 oz (30 g) flesh-colored fondant
Black and green food color gels
1 strand raw, uncooked spaghetti

Equipment
10 in (25 cm) round cake board
Carving knife
Palette knife
Rolling pin
Cake smoothers (optional)
Small, sharp, non-serrated knife
Medium and fine paintbrushes
Toothpick
Pastry bag (optional) see "Tips"

How to Make Your Pony Cake

1 Level the top of the cake and turn it upside down. Slice it horizontally and fill with buttercream. Reassemble and place in the center of the cake board. Spread a coating of buttercream over the top and sides of the cake. Keep the leftover buttercream for the grass later.

2 Knead and roll out 1 pound 12 ounces (800 g) of white fondant. Lift it over the cake and smooth the top and sides. Trim and neaten around the base and keep the excess for covering the board.

3 Moisten the exposed cake board and cover with white fondant using the bandage method shown on page 26.

4 To make the pony, start with the legs. Roll 1¹/₂ ounces (45 g) of dark brown fondant into a sausage about 3¹/₈ inches (8 cm) long. Slice into four equal sections and stand them in a square formation on the top of the cake. Dab a little water on the top of each leg.

5 Roll about 2¹/₂ ounces (75 g) of dark brown fondant into an oval for the body and stick on top of the legs.

6 Make a tiny orange fondant carrot shape for the carrot and place to one side.

7 Roll about ²/₃ ounce (20 g) of dark brown fondant into an oval for the head and stick on the front of the body. Holding your knife horizontal, make a partial cut into the lower part of the horse's head for his mouth. Dab a little water inside the horse's mouth. Insert the carrot and close the mouth around it.

8 Poke two nostrils into the horse's nose with a toothpick.

9 Make two tiny brown triangle shapes for the horse's ears. Indent each ear using the end of a paintbrush and stick onto the head.

10 Make two small white icing ovals for the eyes. Flatten both ovals and stick onto the head.

11 To make the saddle, knead ¹/₂ ounce (15 g) of

black and ¹/₂ ounce (15 g) of brown fondant together. Moisten the horse's back. Roll ¹/₈ ounce (5 g) of this darker fondant into an oval shape. Flatten it with a rolling pin and drape over the horse's back.

12 Mold a further ¹/₈ ounce (5 g) of the dark brown fondant into a thick, flat lozenge shape for the saddle seat and stick it in place. Wrap up and keep the remaining dark brown fondant.

13 Roll 1 ounce (30 g) of white fondant into a sausage about 7 inches (18 cm) long for the rider's legs. Flatten the two ends and bend into "L" shapes for the feet. Lay and stick over the horse's back so that the knees bend slightly and the feet rest on the ground.

14 Make a ¹/₃ ounce (10 g) of red fondant oval for the rider's body. To make it more stable, insert a bit of spaghetti, leaving about ³/₄ inch (2 cm) protruding.

15 Make a ¹/₃-ounce (10 g) flesh-colored ball for the rider's head and slice a little off the top to make it flat for her hat. Stick the head on top of the body.

16 Roll ¹/₃ ounce (10 g) of red fondant into a sausage about 3¹/₂ inches (9 cm) long. Cut it in half and using the rounded ends to form the shoulders, stick one on either side of the body.

17 Use the remaining very dark brown fondant to make the mane. Thinly roll out about ¹/₃ ounce (10 g) and cut out two rectangles. Cut a fringe along one side of each rectangle and stick on the horse's neck. Cut out a few extra tiny strips and lay between the ears.

18 Roll a little dark brown fondant into a thin string about 5 inches (12 cm) long for the reins. Lay and stick the reins in place, from one edge of the horse's mouth, over the horse's neck to the other side of the mouth. Trim to fit if necessary.

19 Shape about ¹/₈ ounce (5 g) of dark brown

fondant into a tapering cone shape for the horse's tail. Press a few lines down its length using the back of a knife. Stick the tail in place.

20 Make two pea-sized balls of flesh-colored fondant for the hands. Stick them on the ends of the arms on top of the reins. Stick a tiny flesh-colored ball on the front of the face for a nose. Add two tiny flattened white fondant balls for eyes.

21 To make the girl's hair, thinly roll out about ¹/₃ ounce (10 g) of brown fondant and cut out two small triangles. Press lines down the length and stick one on either side of the head. Make two smaller triangles and stick against side of the head, resting on the shoulders. Make two tiny white fondant ovals and stick over the joins.

22 Roll ¹/₈ ounce (5 g) of black fondant into a rounded oval shape for the hat. Flatten the base and pinch a brim into the front of the helmet. Stick it onto the rider's head.

23 Place a little black food color gel into a saucer and using a fine brush, paint a dot on each eye. Paint a line across the horse's forehead, one across his nose and one on either side of his head to form the bridle.

24 Paint a few lines around each horse's hoof, draw the girl's mouth and blacken the girl's boots.

25 Dab a little watered down green food coloring on the top of the cake around the horse and rider.

26 Color 2 tablespoons of buttercream green and place in a pastry bag. Close the bag and snip a tiny triangle off the end. Pipe grass around the base and top edge of cake. To do this, place the tip of the bag on the cake, squeeze a little icing out and pull away allowing the icing to form a tail. Also, pipe a tiny tail on the carrot.

Pony Cupcakes

Spread a little apricot jam over the top of the cupcake and place a brown fondant disc on the top. Make a horse's head as described but leave off the bridle.

TIPS: If you don't want to pipe grass, look at the grass on the Crazy Cars Cake on page 40 and smear "grass" around the edges instead.

Or avoid grass altogether and simply put a bright ribbon around the cake instead.

Playful Puppy Cupcakes

The puppies are in three different positions—playful, resting and digging and have three different expressions. This gives you nine different puppies to play with.

I can't really tell you what breed they are—a sort of sugar frosting cross breed!

Makes 9 cupcakes

Ingredients
9 cupcakes
1 quantity buttercream (see page 22)
Confectioners' sugar for rolling out fondant on
Water, boiled and cooled, for sticking
14 oz (400 g) white fondant
4 oz (120 g) black fondant
1/3 oz (10 g) pink fondant
Green and black food color gels

Equipment
Fine and medium paintbrushes
Piping nozzle (tip), circle cutter or small lid
Small, sharp, non-serrated knife
Spoon
Fork

TIP: This design also works well with chocolate buttercream because it looks like mud!

These puppies also look great on large iced birthday cakes.

To Make Your Playful Puppy Cupcakes

1 Make a 1-ounce (30 g) cone shape for the body. Slightly flatten the narrow end to form the front of the puppy.

2 Using a piping nozzle (tip), circle cutter or lid, press two semi-circles into the rear of the puppy.

3 Make two tiny, white fondant ovals for his front paws and stick on the front of the puppy. Press a couple of lines into the front of each paw with the back of your knife.

4 Make two tiny sausage shapes for his rear legs and stick one on either side of his body. Press lines into the front of each paw.

5 To make his head, roll 1/3 ounce (10 g) of white fondant into a cone shape. Stick it on top of the body with the widest part at the front, forming the nose.

6 For the ears, make two tiny black sausage shapes and flatten them. Stick one on either side of the head.

7 Make two or three tiny, black fondant balls and flatten them. Stick one or two on the eye area and one on his back.

8 Make a tiny, black string for the tail and a tiny oval for the nose. Stick both in place.

9 Make two tiny, white fondant ball shapes for the eyes and stick onto the face.

10 Paint two black dots on the eyes and a curved or wavy line or dot for a mouth.

11 Add a tiny pink oval for a tongue if you wish.

Resting Pup

1 Make a 1-ounce (30 g) white fondant cone shape for the body and lay it flat.

2 Press a semi-circle into one side with a lid or circle cutter.

3 Make a 1/2-ounce (15 g) white fondant cone shape for the head and stick onto the front of the body. The widest part should form the nose.

4 Make features as before and a thin fondant string for his tail. Stick this around the base of the body.

Digging Puppy

1 Make a 1-ounce (30 g) white fondant cone shape for the body and using a small circle cutter or lid, press two semi-circles into the rear of the body.

2 Make two small, white fondant sausage shapes for his rear legs and stick them against his body. Press a couple of lines into the front of each paw with the back of a knife.

3 Make two slightly longer white fondant sausage shapes about 3/4 inch (2 cm) long for the front paws. Bend them slightly at the elbows and stick against the front of the dog. Press a couple of lines into the front of each paw as before.

4 Finish off with at black spot on the back and a tail as before.

Assembling the Cupcakes

Place a good spoonful of green-colored buttercream on top of each cupcake and rough it up a little with a fork to look like grass. Place a puppy on top.

Autumn Foliage Cake

The dark brown fondant used to cover this cake works incredibly well with the warm colors of the leaves. To give your cake an added chocolate kick, cover the cake using a chocolate-flavored covering paste (use it in exactly the same way you would fondant) or knead some cocoa powder into 2 pounds 4 ounces (1 kg) marzipan and use that instead.

Ingredients

7 in (18 cm) round sponge cake
1 quantity buttercream (see page 22)
Confectioners' sugar for rolling out
    fondant on
Water, boiled and cooled, for sticking
2 lb 4 oz (1 kg) dark brown-colored
    fondant
Tiny bit of pink-colored fondant (knead a
    tiny bit of red and white together)
7 oz (200 g) white fondant
2 oz (60 g) red fondant
8 oz (250 g) yellow fondant
8 oz (250 g) orange-colored fondant
8 oz (250 g) golden brown-colored
    fondant (see "TIPS")
Black food color gel

Equipment

10 in (25 cm) round cake board
Carving knife
Palette knife
Rolling pin
Cake smoothers (optional)
Pastry brush
Small, soft paintbrush
Small, sharp, non-serrated knife
Toothpick
Leaf templates (see page 78)

TIPS: I colored the golden leaves using a color called "Autumn Leaves." Alternatively knead some orange, yellow and brown food color gel into some white fondant.

Don't try and clean dusty confectioners' sugar smudges off your cake until you have finished the whole cake. Wipe them away with a soft damp brush and allow to dry.

To Make Your Autumn Foliage Cake

1 Level your cake and turn it upside down. Slice and fill it with buttercream. Place it in the center of the board and coat the outsides of the cake with buttercream.

2 Knead and roll out the dark brown fondant

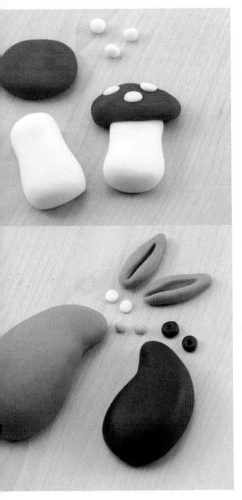

and cover the cake. Smooth the top and sides and trim away the excess from the base.

3 To cover the base, first "paint" a little water around the exposed cake board using a pastry brush. Knead and roll the leftover brown fondant into a long sausage. Flatten into a strip and cover the board using the bandage method shown on page 26. Keep the excess fondant for the animals later.

4 For the toadstools, roll five small 1/3–2/3-ounce (10–20 g) lumps of white fondant into short stumpy sausage shapes. Stand them upright and flatten the tops.

5 Make five red 1/8–1/3-ounce (5–10 g) fondant balls for the toadstool tops and flatten slightly. Stick a top onto each base with a light dab of water. Finish each toadstool with 2 or 3 tiny flattened white balls of fondant and place to one side.

6 For the mice, make two 1-ounce (30 g) brown fondant cone shapes. Bend the tip forward slightly to form the head. Holding your knife vertically, press a small line into the lower part of the head to form his mouth.

7 Make two tiny brown ball shapes for ears and stick onto the head. Poke the end of your paintbrush into each one to make a small hollow. Make a tiny pink ball for each nose and dip a cocktail stick into some black food coloring and make two dots for the eyes. Place to one side.

8 For the rabbit, knead about 1/3 ounce (10 g) of dark brown fondant into 2 ounces (60 g) of white to make a lighter brown color. Pull a little off for the ears and shape the rest into a cone shape. Bend the head forwards slightly and make a small vertical cut for the mouth. Pinch the ends of the ears into points and stick

on top of the rabbit's head.

9 Add a tiny pink nose and two flattened white ball shapes for eyes. Add two dots for eyes using black food coloring.

10 Arrange and stick the mice, toadstools and rabbit around the cake with dabs of water

11 To make the leaves, thinly roll out some of the yellow fondant. Holding your knife almost vertical, which makes it easier, cut out two or three leaf shapes. Press a few veins into them and drape and stick onto the cake. Reuse the leftover fondant.

12 Repeat using a different color and continue until the top and board are covered with leaves.

Autumn Cupcakes

Spread a little chocolate buttercream "mud" over the top of the cupcake. Make a toadstool and a couple of leaves as shown above and place on top of the cake.

Soccer Player Cake

By changing the color of the player's uniform, hair style and skin tone you can easily adapt this player and his uniform to match those of a favorite team and player.

Ingredients
7 in (18 cm) square sponge cake
1 quantity buttercream (see page 22)
Confectioners' sugar for rolling out
    fondant on
Water, boiled and cooled, for sticking
2 lb 4 oz (1 kg) green-colored fondant
5 oz (150 g) white fondant
1/2 oz (15 g) black fondant
1 oz (30 g) red fondant
1 oz (30 g) flesh-colored fondant

Equipment
10 in (25 cm) round cake board
Carving knife
Palette knife
Tape measure or ruler
Plastic food wrap
Small, sharp, non-serrated knife
Fine and medium soft paintbrushes
Piping nozzle (tip), any design
Fork

TIP If you want to make a less complex soccer cake, simply cover a round or square cake and either make a sitting down character like the football player on page 48, but dress him in a soccer gear, or follow these instructions but with the character laying flat on top of the cake.

Use a chocolate soccerball as the main ball on the cake if you prefer.

Soccer Player Cupcakes

Smear the top of the cupcake with green-colored buttercream and rough the buttercream up with a fork to look like grass. Place a few chocolate or fondant soccerballs on top.

To Make Your Soccer Player Cake

1 Cut the cake to shape by first leveling the top of the cake to make it flat. Then stand it on its side and cut a slope into the top edge. This will form the back of the net.

2 With the cake standing upright, slice the cake horizontally twice into layers, if you wish, and fill it with buttercream. Just be aware that if you do this it will make the cake slightly less secure until it has been covered with fondant and the fondant has had a chance to firm up. So try not to knock it over.

3 Stand the cake towards the rear of the board and spread buttercream over the sides and top. Place a strip of plastic wrap over the front, top and back of the cake but leave the sides exposed. (This will keep the buttercream in these areas soft and tacky while you cover the sides.)

4 Knead and roll out 10 ounces (300 g) of green-colored fondant. Cut out a thick strip and stand against the one of the sides of the goal. Cut around the edges and base and remove the excess. Repeat on the other side.

5 Dab a little water on the exposed edges of the fondant sides. Knead and roll out 1 pound 8 ounces (700 g) of green fondant and cut out a long wide strip the width of the cake and long enough to go over the front, top and back of the cake.

6 Remove the plastic wrap and lay the green fondant over the cake. Trim and neaten the edges and base.

7 To make the goal posts, roll 1 ounce (30 g) of white fondant into a long thin string about 7 inches (18 cm) long. Paint a light line of water along the front top edge of the goal then lay and stick the white string on top of it. Trim the edges to fit in line with the edge of the cake.

8 Paint a line of water along the outside edges of the goal. Make two 1½-ounce (45 g) white fondant strings about 15 inches (38 cm) long. Stick one up the front left hand side of the cake, over the top and down to the base at the back. Repeat on the other side of the cake and trim and neaten the base.

9 Make two ⅛-ounce (5 g) black fondant oval shapes for the player's boots. Place one to one side and stick the other off center on the board against the cake.

10 Roll ⅓ ounce (10 g) of red fondant into an oval about 2 inches (4.5 cm) long for the socks. Cut in half. Place one to one side and stick the other on top of the boot against the side of the cake at a slight angle.

11 Roll ⅓ ounce (10 g) of flesh-colored fondant into a thin string about 5 inches (12 cm) long for his legs. Cut in half and bend both legs into a sort of boomerang shape. Stick one leg on top of the sock against the cake with the knee pointing forwards. Stick the second leg against the top of the first one with the knee pointing upwards. Stick the second sock and boot in position against the cake.

12 Thinly roll out about ⅓ ounce (10 g) of white fondant for the shorts. Cut out two rectangles about ½ x 1 inch (1.5 x 2.5 cm). Stick one rectangle horizontally on top of the outstretched leg. Stick the second vertically on top of the player's standing leg.

13 Roll ⅛ ounce (5 g) of red fondant into an oval for the player's body and flatten it. Stick it on top of the shorts against the cake.

14 Roll about ⅛ ounce (5 g) of red fondant into a thin string about 3 inches (8 cm) long for the arms. Cut in half and bend each arm at the elbow. Stick onto the cake. Stick a small, flattened ball of flesh-colored fondant on the end of each arm for the hands.

15 Roll about ⅛ ounce (5 g) of flesh-colored fondant into an oval for the head. Squash it slightly and stick on top of the body against the cake.

16 Make him smile by holding a piping nozzle (tip) at an angle, then press it into the lower part of his face and pull it downwards slightly. This should leave an exaggerated smiling "U" impression in the fondant.

17 Add two tiny, flesh-colored ball shapes—one for his ear and one for his nose. Press a little hollow into the ear with the end of your paintbrush. Make and stick two tiny, white ball shapes for his eyes.

18 To make the hair, dip about ⅛ ounce (5 g) of black fondant into water and work it between your fingers until it's sticky. Place on top of the head and tweak into position.

19 Make a ⅛-ounce (5 g) white fondant disc for the ball and stick onto the cake (see "Tip"). Paint a pattern on the ball with black food color and a black dot on each eye. Paint a few lines to represent the net onto the goal.

20 Color the leftover buttercream green and spread around the board. Use a fork to make it look like grass. Sprinkle a few wrapped chocolate soccerballs around the grass if you wish.

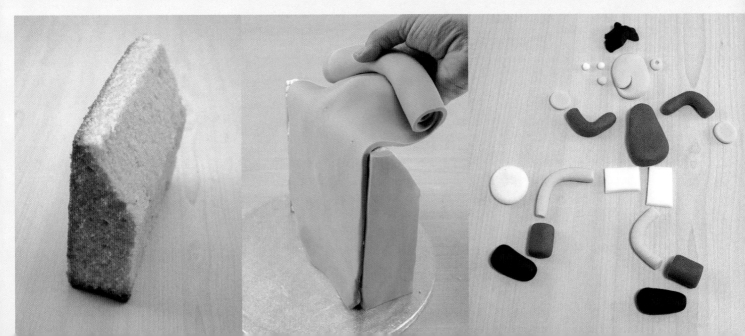

Smelly Sneaker Cake

After opening the shoe cupboard at home recently I know this cake would suit a few people in my house! Although the sneaker harbors horrors such as rats, flies and maggots, the cake itself should taste really good!

Ingredients

Cake baked in a loaf pan (see page 16)
1 quantity buttercream (see page 22)
Confectioners' sugar for rolling out fondant on
Water, boiled and cooled, for sticking
1 lb 12 oz (800 g) white fondant
1 oz (30 g) green fondant
3½ oz (100 g) black fondant
⅓ oz (10 g) brown fondant
1 sheet edible wafer paper
Black, green, and brown food color gels
2½ oz (75 g) green-colored desiccated coconut (see page 27)
1 pack laces sweets
2 jelly snakes

Equipment

10 in (25 cm) round cake board
Carving knife
Palette knife
Rolling pin
Small, sharp, non-serrated knife
Fine and medium paintbrushes
Shoe and wing templates (see pages 78 & 79)
Pencil
Scissors

> **TIP:** If you can't get hold of jelly snakes make fondant ones instead.
>
> If you don't like coconut, mix up some chocolate buttercream instead and smear that around the board and shoe. It makes excellent mud!

Sneaker Cupcakes

Spread green colored buttercream over the top of the cupcake and rough it up with a fork to look like grass. Shape about 1 ounce (30 g) of white fondant into an oval for the sneaker. Press a hollow into the top of the shoe using the end of a wooden spoon or bone tool. Press two lines down the front of the sneaker with the back of your knife and a few lines across for laces. Press a line just above the base of the shoe to make the sole. Stick a small disc of black fondant inside the top of the sneaker.

To Make Your Smelly Sneaker Cake

1 Level the top of the cake and turn it upside down so the widest part of the cake forms the base.

2 Carefully carve the cake into shape using the template if necessary. Leaving the height of the ankle section intact, carve a slight slope into the middle third of the trainer. Allow it to taper down and flatten out over the toe area.

3 Split and fill the cake with buttercream. Reassemble it and place in the center of the board. Spread buttercream around the top and sides.

4 Roll 2 ounces (60 g) of white fondant into a sausage shape about 8 inches (20 cm) long. Place it in a circle on top of the ankle section and lightly moisten with a little water.

5 Knead and roll out 1 pound 5 ounces (600 g) of white fondant into a 1/3-inch (1 cm) thick oval shape. Lift and place over the cake. Press the fondant into the ankle area first to avoid air getting caught. Then smooth over the rest of the cake. Trim around the base.

6 Roll out 1 ounce (30 g) of green fondant into a 3-inch (8 cm) sausage. Using a rolling pin, flatten it into a long, flat oval shape about 5 inches (12 cm) long for the shoe's tongue. Stick this onto the front center of the shoe with a little water. The top of the tongue should protrude above the top of the shoe. Using the end of a paintbrush, poke 6 holes for the laces in the white fondant on either side of the green.

7 Roll 1 ounce (30 g) of black fondant into a 3-inch (8 cm) sausage. Flatten it with a rolling pin to make a long strip with rounded ends about 7 inches (18 cm) long. Stick this around the top edge of the toe.

8 Roll about 1 ounce (30 g) of black fondant into a ball. Flatten it into a disc and stick inside the top of the shoe.

9 Roll 1/3 ounce (10 g) of brown fondant into a string about 8 inches (20 cm) long and stick on the board around the front of the shoe. Press vertical lines into it by holding your knife upright.

10 To make the back of the heel, roll 2 1/2 ounces (75 g) of white fondant into a sausage about 8 inches (20 cm) long. Carefully press along one long edge to produce a slope running the whole length of the strip.

11 Lay the strip resting on the board around the heel of the shoe, press vertical lines into it with a knife as before.

12 Roll 1 ounce (30 g) of black fondant into a sausage about 3 1/2 inches (9 cm) long. Flatten it into a long rounded rectangle about 6 inches (15 cm) long. Lay and stick around the back of the heel.

13 Thinly roll out some leftover green and black fondant and cut out two green and two black rectangles and stick onto the sides of the shoe.

14 Cut the long lace sweets into 2 1/2-inch (6 cm) sections. Poke and stick them down the front of the sneaker. Insert two uncut longer "laces" into the top of the shoe to look as though the shoe is undone.

15 To make the rats, knead 1/8 ounce (5 g) of black and 1 1/2 ounces (45 g) of white fondant together to make gray. Place about 1/8 ounce (5 g) to one side and roll the rest into two pointed carrot shapes. Bend the pointed ends forward to form the nose and stick both rats into the top of the shoe.

16 Make 4 tiny ball shapes for ears and stick two on each head. Poke the end of a paintbrush into each ear. Make four tiny tear shapes for paws and two thin gray strings for tails. Press a few lines into each paw with a knife.

17 Cut the jelly snakes to length and arrange and stick the cut ends into the top of the shoe. Stick two tiny white fondant balls on the front of each snake for eyes.

18 To make the flies, make some tiny black fondant ovals and stick onto the trainer. Cut tiny wing shapes out of edible wafer paper and stick two into the top of each fly.

19 For the maggots, knead a little brown into a little white. Make tiny, tapering sausage shapes and press lines across the back of each maggot with the back of your knife. Stick them onto the cake.

20 To finish, paint black food coloring dots on the eyes and the rat's nose's and a few legs on the flies and dab some watered down brown food coloring onto the sneaker to look like mud. Sprinkle the colored coconut "grass" around the board.

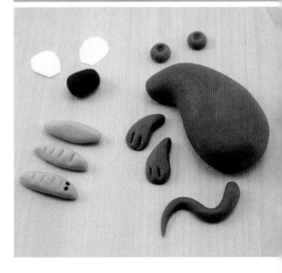

Best Friends Sleepover Cake

This is a very girly girl cake with its pink and purple color scheme, but it would work just as well in shades of green, blue or yellow.

Ingredients
8 x 6 in (20 x 15 cm) rectangular cake
(cut 2 in/5 cm off the side of a
8 in/20 cm square cake)
1 quantity buttercream (see page 22)
Confectioners' sugar for rolling out
fondant on
Water, boiled and cooled, for sticking
1 lb 15 oz (900 g) white fondant
1 lb 2 oz (500 g) purple fondant
1½ oz (45 g) flesh-colored fondant
1 lb (450 g) pink fondant
1 oz (30 g) brown fondant
1 oz (30 g) black fondant
⅔ oz (20 g) yellow fondant
Chocolate finger cookies or similar
1–2 packs of sweets to decorate

Equipment
12 in (30 cm) square cake board
Carving knife
Palette knife
Rolling pin
Small, sharp, non-serrated knife
Cake smoother (optional)
Medium and fine paintbrushes
1½ in (4 cm) diameter circle cutter (optional)
Plastic food wrap

TIP: Use the pets and sweets to hide any tears in the bedding or unsightly joints in the carpet.
A messy unmade bed cake with no one in it would also make a fun cake for someone who has "problems" remembering to make their bed in the mornings!

Sleepover Cupcakes

Spread apricot jam over the top of the cupcake. Place a flat white fondant disc on top. Make a white rectangle for the pillow. Make a flesh-colored ball for the head and stick it on top of the pillow. Use a drinking straw to make two "U"-shaped eyes and add a tiny flesh ball for the nose. Add a few thin brown fondant strings for her hair. Stick a small oval of white fondant on the top of the cake for her body. Make a thin pink fondant semi-circle for the blanket, then cut out a thin white strip for the sheet and stick along the top of the blanket over the lower part of the girl's face.

To Make Your Sleepover Cake

1 Level the cake and turn it upside down. Split and fill it with buttercream and place towards the top left hand corner of the cake board. Buttercream the sides and top.

2 Knead 1 pound 2 ounces (500 g) of white fondant until soft. Roll it out and cover the cake. Smooth the sides and trim and neaten the base.

3 Lightly moisten the exposed cake board with a little water. Knead and thinly roll out 1 pound 2 ounces (500 g) of purple fondant. Cut 4 strips and lay over the board. Smooth into place and cut to fit. Neaten the joins and the edges. Keep the excess fondant (you should have about 10 ounces/300 g leftover).

4 Make two thick 2-ounce (60 g) white fondant rectangles for pillows. Pinch each corner into a point and stick at the head of the bed, but don't let them overhang the back.

5 To make girl one's (Fig.1) head, roll $\frac{1}{2}$ ounce (15 g) of pink flesh-colored fondant into a ball. Poke the end of a paintbrush into the lower part of the head to make her mouth. Stick the head on the left hand side of the pillows. Make a $1\frac{1}{2}$-ounce (45 g) white sausage shape for her body. Bend the end up to give the impression of feet and lay and stick it on top of the bed.

6 Make two tiny, white balls for her eyes. Flatten them and stick them on her head. Roll out a little yellow fondant and press lines down its length. Cut out a small rectangle and a simple leaf shape. Place the leaf shape to one side and cover with plastic wrap to stop it from drying out. Lay the rectangle over the top of her head.

7 Make two flesh-colored balls for her ears and a smaller one for her nose. Stick all three in place and press the end of a paintbrush into each ear to leave a small hollow.

8 To make girl two's (Fig. 2) body, roll 1 ounce (30 g) of pink fondant into an oval and stick onto the bed. Poke some hollows with the end of a paintbrush to look like spots. Roll $\frac{1}{2}$ ounce (15 g) of brown-colored fondant into a ball for her head and stick on top of the pink. Add eyes and a nose.

9 Roll $\frac{1}{3}$ ounce (10 g) of pink fondant into a sausage about 4 inches (10 cm) long and cut in two for her arms. Using the rounded ends for the shoulders, stick the two arms in place. The wrists should rest on girl one's head. Decorate with "spots" as before.

10 Make two small brown ball shapes for hands and stick on the end of the arms with the yellow leaf shape between them.

11 Thinly roll out about $\frac{1}{2}$ ounce (15 g) of black fondant and press lines across its length. Cut out a circle about $1\frac{1}{2}$ inches (4 cm) across and cut in half. Stick on top of girl two's head. Cut two flat triangles out of the remaining black and stick against girl two's head to form pigtails. Stick two tiny purple ovals over the joins.

12 Make a 1-ounce (30 g) purple oval shape for girl three's (Fig.3) body and stick onto the bed. Make a $\frac{1}{2}$-ounce (15 g) flesh-colored ball for her head and stick on top of the body.

13 Make a bowl by rolling $\frac{2}{3}$ ounce (20 g) of yellow fondant into a cone shape. Flatten the two ends and stick the widest part upright against girl three's body. Tear a little white fondant into tiny pieces and stick on top of the yellow to look like popcorn. Stick two tiny, white, flattened ball shapes on the face for her eyes.

14 Make a $\frac{1}{3}$-ounce (10 g) purple fondant sausage and cut in half to make two purple arms. Stick one around the bowl and the other bent at the elbow with the wrist up near the face.

15 Make two small flesh-colored ball shapes for her hands and stick on the ends of her arms. Make a tiny flesh ball for her nose and stick on her face. Stick a few bits of white around the hand on the mouth to look like popcorn.

16 To make the sleeping bag, roll out and cut about $3\frac{1}{2}$ ounces (100 g) of pink fondant into a 6-inch (15 cm) square. Fold the bag in half and press lines down and across it with the back of your knife. Fold the top corner back onto itself. Make a $\frac{1}{2}$-ounce (15 g) white rectangular pillow and slip into the top of the bag. Stick the sleeping bag on the floor next to the bed.

17 To make the bed covers, knead and roll out 7 ounces (200 g) of white fondant and cut out a rectangle about 12 x $3\frac{1}{8}$ inches (30 x 8 cm). Place to one side and cover with plastic wrap. Roll out 10 ounces (300 g) of pink fondant and cut out a square about 10 x 10 inches (25 x 25 cm). Paint a line of water along the bottom edge of the white fondant and rest one edge of the pink square on top.

18 Fold the white back towards and over the pink so it looks like a sheet over a blanket. Lift the bedding up and arrange over the bed.

19 Make a dog and cat if you wish (see puppy and kitty cupcake instructions)

20 Paint pupils on all the eyes and a mouth on girl two and arrange sweets around the cake and board. "Glue" a line of cookies behind the bed with buttercream to make the headboard.

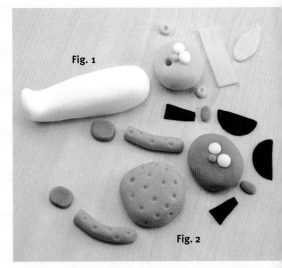

Fig. 1

Fig. 2

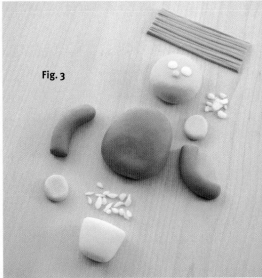

Fig. 3

Templates (all templates actual size)

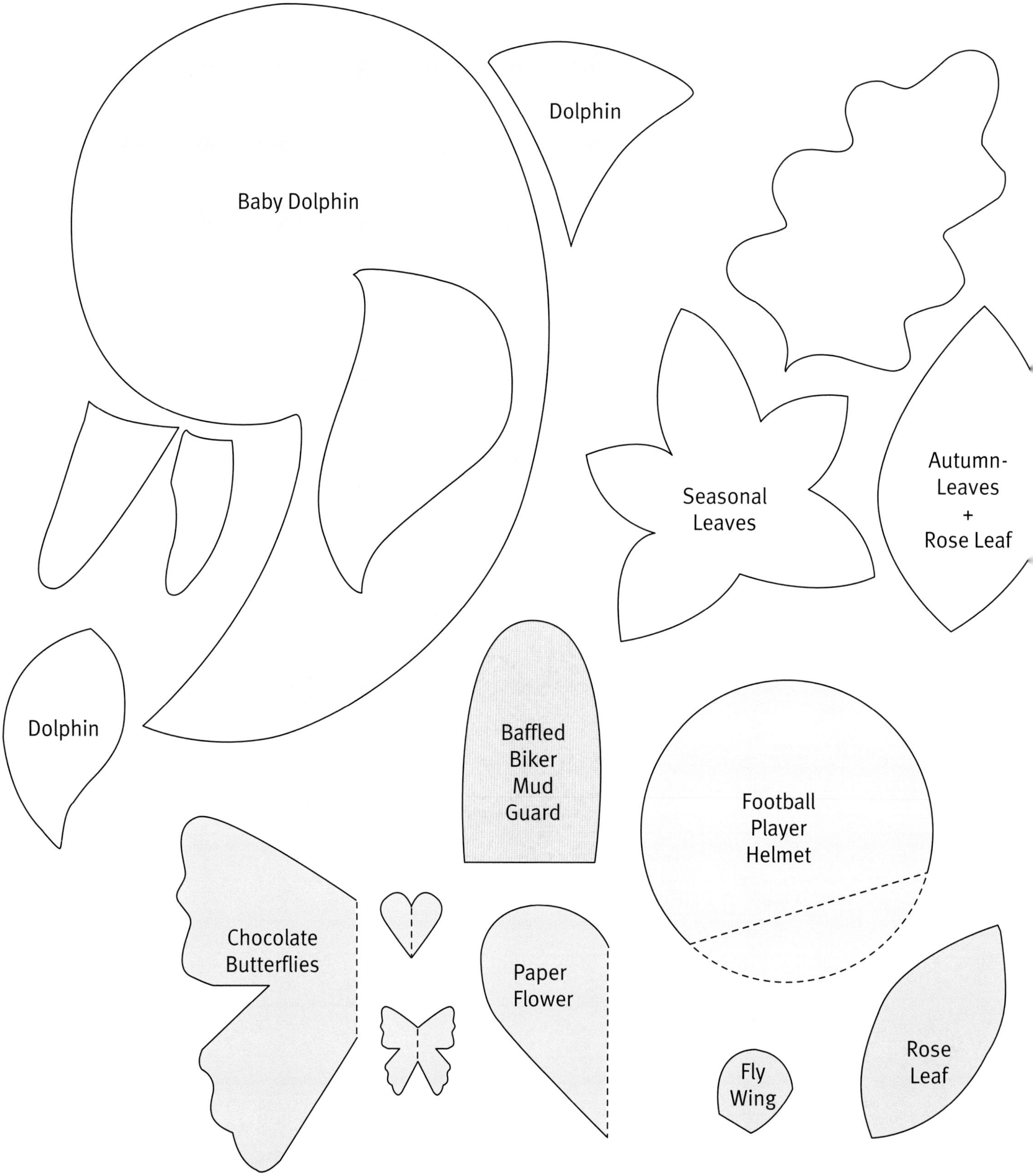

Dolphin

Baby Dolphin

Seasonal Leaves

Autumn-Leaves + Rose Leaf

Dolphin

Baffled Biker Mud Guard

Football Player Helmet

Chocolate Butterflies

Paper Flower

Fly Wing

Rose Leaf

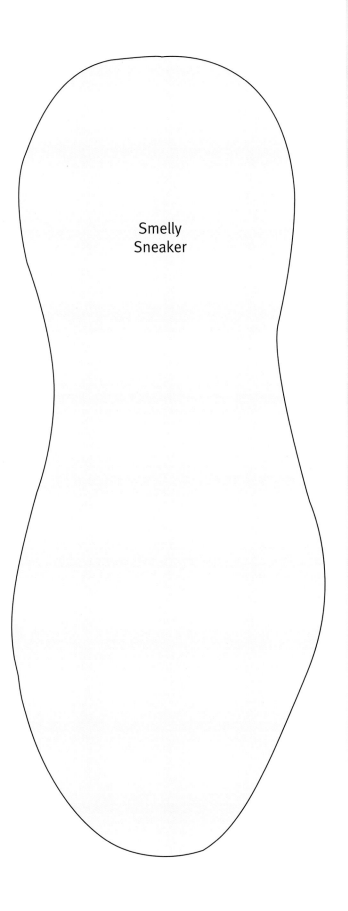

Smelly
Sneaker

Making a Piping Bag

1 Make a greaseproof paper triangle and lay it flat with the point towards you. Fold "C" over to form a cone shape.

2 Wrap "A" around the cone. Points "A" and "C" should meet together at the back and the tip of the cone should be pointed.

3 Fold "A" and "C" over a couple of times to hold the bag together. If using a piping nozzle (tip) cut a little off the point and place the nozzle (tip) inside followed by some buttercream. If you are not using a nozzle just place buttercream inside the bag. Fold the top over to close the bag and cut a tiny triangle off the point ready for piping.

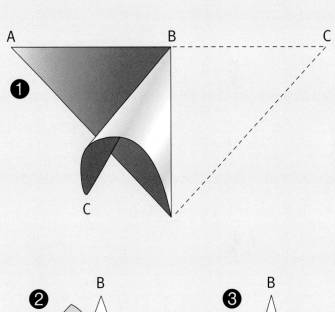

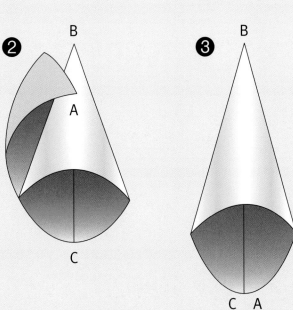

Suppliers

If you have trouble obtaining cake equipment or materials including fondant (sugarpaste) one of the following companies may be able to help.

UK

Culpitt Ltd
Jubilee Industrial Estate
Ashington
Northumberland
NE63 8UQ
UK
Tel: +44 (0) 1670 814545
www.culpitt.com

Design a Cake
30 / 31 Phoenix Road,
Crowther Industrial Estate,
Washington,
Tyne & Wear,
NE38 0AD
UK
Sales: +44(0)191 417 1572
Enquiries +44(0) 1914179697
www.design-a-cake.co.uk

Renshawnapier Limited
Crown street
Liverpool
L8 7RF
Tel 0151 706 8200
www.renshawnapier.co.uk

Squires Kitchen
3 Waverley Lane
Farnham
Surrey
GU9 8BB
UK
Tel: +44 (0)1252 260 260
www.squires-shop.com

USA

Beryl's Cake Decorating & Pastry Supplies
PO Box 1584
North Springfield, VA 22151
Tel: 1-800-488-2749
Fax: (703) 750-3779
www.beryls.com

Wilton
Wilton Industries
2240 W 75th St
Woodridge
IL 60517
Tel: 630-963-1818 or
800-794-5866
www.wilton.com

If you have any problems or get stuck contact me:
http://caroldeaconcakes.com

Index